I've worked with the authors and as a consequence know that their advice is based on huge experience and rigour. They write as they talk: common sense supported by acute observation.
Sir John Rose, former CEO, Rolls-Royce (1996–2011)

Having worked with both authors, I am continually struck by the impact that their methodology has on senior leaders. Their approach is both provocative and pragmatic and has led to some amazing experiment results.

Following the pandemic, our organization has entered a phase where experimentation is ever more critical. Leaders now know very clearly that the future is uncertain and nobody has the perfect answer. We can only find the answers through exploration and experimentation if we are to innovate and thrive in the new world. Creating a culture where this is not just encouraged but seen as essential will become a key differentiator of organizational resilience and performance.
Roger Minton, Head of Leadership Development, Anglo American

In today's volatile and uncertain world, experimentation is the best way to test assumptions and respond quickly to changes. Rob James and Jules Goddard have been teaching the 'how to' of experimentation to executives for the past two decades. They have now put their insights and wisdom into this practical and very readable book. It is a winner! It belongs on the shelf of every manager.
Costas Markides, Professor of Strategy and Entrepreneurship, London Business School

Competent managers deliver on the promise; they follow processes, simply put, and they play the game well. Exceptional leaders on the other hand, challenge the status quo; they dream big, take bold risks, ignite a movement. They 'create a new game'.

Rob James and Jules Goddard in *Business Experimentation* provide a fresh and innovative perspective of this notion of change, and the role of experimentation in triggering transformational change. Based on my first-hand experience as a participant in Randstad's Transformational Leadership Programme, it is clear that under Rob and Jules' guidance, the experimentation movement has changed our game. In fact, it has become a key part of ensuring that our organization is future-ready.
Paul Dupuis, CEO, Randstad Japan

In partnership with London Business School, and with the authors playing a key role, we co-designed a programme to prepare our leaders for transformation. By creating connections, building networks and using experiments as a catalyst for change, the programme has contributed to Randstad becoming the world market leader in our industry.
Jos Schut, Chief Human Resources Officer, Randstad

Most seasoned executives buy into the idea that we should encourage more experimentation in business, but they often don't know where to start. This book solves the problem – it is full of practical advice, and it is written by two genuine experts who have been helping organizations run business experiments for more than a decade.
Julian Birkinshaw, Professor of Strategy and Entrepreneurship, London Business School

I have greatly enjoyed learning with Jules Goddard over the last several years in the Academic Council of CEDEP at Fontainebleau. He and Rob James have written an exceptional book focusing on the importance of experimentation in business.

The world's biggest innovations and discoveries have been made as a result of thoughtful experiments, observations with mindfulness and learning from what worked and what did not. This requires us to foster curiosity, the spirit of adventure and the courage to formulate new hypotheses that challenge conventional wisdom, embrace failure and learn.

Jules and Rob have rich experience gained through twelve years of facilitating experiments in several business organizations and have acquired deep insights as a result. Their writing is a dance between philosophical gems and practical nuggets and readers are stimulated to think about how they could embark on their own journeys of experimentation.

Anil Sachdev, Founder and Chairman, School of Inspired Leadership, India

This is a deeply insightful, thought-provoking and practical book, offering an approach that will be of value to organizations of all kinds. The authors unpack experimentation with commendable clarity.

Dr Andrew MacLennan, Founder and Managing Director, Strategy Execution Ltd

Could there be a timelier book than *Business Experimentation*! As businesses the world over look to reset, I doubt there can be a more important guide for leaders to read. This book will expand thinking, inspire action and provide the courage and know-how to challenge business orthodoxies and assumptions that are in urgent need of such. *Business Experimentation* provides a cornerstone for any leader or organization intent on understanding what it will take to thrive in our uncertain and complex world. It is a book that will help shape and define your future.

Keith Coats, futurist and leadership expert, and Co-founder of TomorrowToday Global

This book boldly invites us to become 'experimentalists'.

As we make the unprecedented global transition to a so-called 'new normal' in a post-pandemic world, there has never been a better time for leaders to embrace the essential qualities of experimentation as a powerful tool for innovation and transformation. Too often, we remain overly reliant on our prior experience and assumptions to make important decisions in an increasingly uncertain world. But as the authors show, experimentation provides an emergent, relevant and vastly more powerful tool to navigate complexity.

Jules Goddard and Rob James build on their excellent prior writings about business, strategy and creativity to provide a practical approach that will be refreshing and immediately useful to leaders at any level. Importantly, the authors also widen the aperture to the organizational and even societal level to ask what makes a culture of experimentation, how this benefits us, and how to drive this more deliberately as leaders. Finally, they challenge our assumptions about what areas of business can benefit from experimentation, and in the process prove that the field of play is far more vast than we might have believed.

For anyone interested in exploring the spirit of experimentation in their organization, and building a culture of curiosity for themselves, this will be essential reading.

Andy Craggs, The Jump Network – specialists in strategic leadership for organizational performance

All great businesses start as successful experiments. For some strange reason, they then choose to abandon the very approach that made them successful in the first place. They get taken over by a caste who can claim credit for cost savings and efficiencies, without ever being held responsible for missed opportunities. This book is a celebration of a truly scientific approach to business, one that seeks to find out what you don't know, rather than endlessly optimizing on the little that you do.

Rory Sutherland, Vice Chairman, Ogilvy UK, TEDGlobal speaker, and author of *Alchemy: The surprising power of ideas that don't make sense*

This book is a perfect balance of academic rigour *and* business relevance. It is provocative and provides pragmatic tools for success that explain the Why, the What and the How. It has been an inspiring learning journey and a delight to work with the authors, who are driven by a genuine intent to make a difference in shaping individual and organizational growth.

Linda Irwin, Senior Client Director, London Business School

With increasing global pressure on organizations to evolve and win at pace, experimentation is going to be key to organizational success.

Experimentation, by its nature, is for some organizations counter to current cultural norms where failure, mistakes and poor decisions are frowned upon, and yet the ability of an organization to try things out and be curious as to how decisions and ideas develop can be central to its survival. Applying experimentation is a way of lightening the burden on organizations to 'always get things right' and in doing so create more opportunities to succeed. In this highly practical book, Jules Goddard and Rob James outline what it takes to bring experimentation to life, to have fun and increase an organization's curiosity in finding what works and adds value and what doesn't, and celebrate the fact that it doesn't. Having worked with Jules on the topic of experimentation on our Senior Leadership Programmes, I can attest to his magical way of inviting more interest and play in bringing greater ideas to the fore through the art of experimentation. This is a vital business book that has arrived at the right time.
Steve Hurst, VP Learning and Development, Sage

Business Experimentation is very timely. There is a sense of urgency to do things differently; therefore organizations must build a strong capability to develop and test alternatives. Jules Goddard and Rob James' book provides a high-level reflection and a practical road map to experiment and find new ways forward.
Muriel Larvaron, Director, Insights and Partnerships, CEDEP, Fontainebleau, France

In our increasingly complex and changing world, leaders need to be more curious, inquire continuously into the evolution of their organizations and their ecosystem, and take courageous steps forward. Deliberate experimentation offers a safe enough 'try-out-and-learn' process to explore 'future-proof' strategies and uncommon, distinctive practices. In my work with Jules Goddard to support Danone executives in their development, I learned the power of business experiments, inviting them to try out and share new paths – some in the area of strategy, others to evolve their ways of working, and many in their own leadership – and observing most of them enlightened by the passion of discovery, often co-creating fresh business ideas for Danone. This book offers a wise reflection as well as a practical approach to make business experiments part of the way we lead our organizations into the future.

Thierry Bonetto, former Director of Learning and Development, Danone (2008–2018)

As a senior executive, I have been moved and inspired by the shared success of various companies' employee communities. I have spent years asking myself the question, 'How can I create the best conditions in order for people within the organization to find their way, their place and to flourish, individually and collectively, all the while adapting to a rapid and ever-changing environment?'

Business Experimentation is a great source of insight for leaders who understand that the world is ever-changing and consistently strive to master this and to adapt. It is for leaders who develop organizations with a culture of continuous improvement and who strongly believe in engaging their employees to succeed, while delivering the company strategy. This book is also a wonderful opportunity for leaders who exert themselves to create the necessary conditions to allow their employees to find their way, to trust themselves and reach their fullest potential. Finally, it is for leaders who acknowledge that they live in a world of uncertainty and that every step is a learning curve, an experiment and an opportunity to grow.

This is not for leaders who don't ask to be questioned and who believe that they never make mistakes!

Pierre Deheunynck, former Executive Vice President and former Head of Human Resources, Transformation and Global Business Support, ENGIE Group (2016–2020)

The current pandemic challenges us and demands experimentation with new ways of doing things. Rob James and Jules Goddard provide here, in a brilliant way, their vast expertise and experience on business experimentation. This book is a truly motivational guide to dare more, to experiment more and to innovate more, for better solutions in today's complex world. You will be inspired and excited as you read Rob and Jules' book and will immediately feel like starting your own experiments.

Dr Sven Ebert, Head of Innovation Laboratory, Roche Diagnostics International

Business Experimentation

A practical guide for driving innovation and performance in your business

Rob James

Jules Goddard

KoganPage

First published in Great Britain and the United States in 2021 by Kogan Page Limited

2nd Floor, 45 Gee Street
London
EC1V 3RS
United Kingdom
www.koganpage.com

122 W 27th St, 10th Floor
New York, NY 10001
USA

4737/23 Ansari Road
Daryaganj
New Delhi 110002
India

Kogan Page books are printed on paper from sustainable forests.

ISBNs

Hardback   978 1 3986 0170 3
Paperback   978 1 3986 0167 3
eBook   978 1 3986 0168 0

British Library Cataloguing-in-Publication Data
A CIP record for this book is available from the British Library.

Library of Congress Cataloging-in-Publication Data
Names: James, Rob (Management consultant), author. | Goddard, Jules, author.
Title: Business experimentation : a practical guide for driving innovation and performance in your business / Rob James, Jules Goddard.
Description: London ; New York, NY : Kogan Page, 2021. | Includes bibliographical references and index. |
Identifiers: LCCN 2021026292 (print) | LCCN 2021026293 (ebook) | ISBN 9781398601673 (paperback) | ISBN 9781398601703 (hardback) | ISBN 9781398601680 (ebook)
Subjects: LCSH: Organizational change. | Organizational behavior. | Business planning. | Strategic planning.
Classification: LCC HD58.8 .J35 2021 (print) | LCC HD58.8 (ebook) | DDC 658.4/06–dc23

Typeset by Integra Software Services, Pondicherry
Print production managed by Jellyfish
Printed and bound by CPI Group (UK) Ltd, Croydon CR0 4YY

CONTENTS

- The following online resources (available for download at **www.koganpage.com/BusExp**) accompany this book:

- OR0: Introduction to experimentation

- OR1: Opportunities for experimentation (large organizations)

- OR1a: Opportunities for experimentation (SMEs)

- OR2: Identify – how to run a SWOT–PESTLE workshop (organization)

- OR2a: Identify – how to run a SWOT–PESTLE workshop (SME)

- OR3: Topic selection workshop (operational)

- OR4: Ideation – freethinking exercise

- OR5: Filtering and prioritizing ideas

- OR6: Formulating a hypothesis

- OR7: Managing risk and complexity

- OR8: Topic selection criteria (manageability)

- OR9: Assessing scientific rigour

- OR10: Monitoring and review processes

- OR11: Structuring the recommendations

- OR12: Organizational assessment questionnaire

- OR13: Personal assessment competences and questionnaire

- OR14: Personal experiment guide and comparator

FOREWORD

Experimentation is disciplined play. The playfulness consists in having ideas; the discipline consists in testing them. An experimental culture is one that places greater weight on the invention of break-through ideas than the implementation of worthy plans. In a choice between a good idea badly executed and a bad idea well executed, the business experimentalist will opt for the former. The reality is that most businesses take the opposite point of view. Success is seen to be a return on the application of second-hand strategies rather than the discovery of counterintuitive truths.

In 1903, a young chemist named Martin Rosanoff was recruited by Thomas Edison to join the staff of his celebrated Menlo Park laboratory. Within a day or two of starting work, Rosanoff approached his boss, 'Mr Edison, please tell me what laboratory rules you want me to observe?' Edison, who was chewing tobacco, spat on the floor and yelled, 'Hell! There are no rules here – we're trying to accomplish something!'

Apocryphal or not, the story conveys a truth that is particularly perti-nent to the business world of today. Most large-scale organizations have become choked by self-inflicted rules. Execution takes precedence over exploration. Long ago, Max Weber predicted correctly that bureaucracy, by pursuing efficiency at the cost of democracy, would inevitably lead to what he called an 'iron cage' in which compliance and control rather than conjecture and discovery would hold sway.

Experimentation shows a way out of this cage. Rather than limit the firm to untested, and therefore risk-averse, ideas and initiatives, a culture of experimentation acts as an insurance policy enabling managers to be more imaginative and daring in the strategies they formulate. Knowing that foolhardy ideas will be detected and aban-doned, managers can afford to be more imaginative in the range of ideas they put forward for consideration. The firm no longer limits itself to a small number of rather conventional and safe options; it gives full rein to the discovery of disruptive or counterintuitive ideas that have the potential to revolutionize an industry.

Experimentation is founded on the belief that, in a market economy, the greatest rewards are reserved for those with the imagination and courage to disrupt conventional or obsolete industry practices. In effect, the workplace is transformed into something more akin to Edison's lab, where primacy is given to originality rather than predictability. After all, capitalism only works if the companies that constitute the economy are as clever and courageous as those who work for them. As it is, too many organizations subtract value from the collective talent of their members. Only through systematic and continuous experimentation can organizations learn as fast as change itself.

The call made in this book for greater experimentation is timely. It is a deliberate plea for companies to live up to the wealth-creating responsibilities that an open society and a free economy rightly expect of business; and it puts forward a blueprint for doing so. Over time, by privileging what is true rather than what is convenient, experimentation creates a meritocracy of ideas in place of an autocracy of opinion. For many managers of the old school, what may at first be seen as a pedantic and time-consuming emphasis on controlled testing gradually succumbs to an appreciation of the power of reason and transparency. The baleful grip of managerialism is loosened.

The development of an experimentation culture goes hand in hand with the creation of what I have called a humanocracy. By this I mean a post-managerial form of organization that lives and breathes the higher human faculties of enquiry, ingenuity and initiative. It forms the foundations of a workplace that is fit for the future and fit for human beings.

Gary Hamel
The Wall Street Journal's *No.1 business thinker*

ACKNOWLEDGEMENTS

We have been extraordinarily fortunate over the last few years to have worked with a large number of experimentation teams drawn from some of the world's most enterprising companies, including Bridgestone, Clariant, Danone, Engie, If, KPMG, Randstad, Roche, Sage and Vinci.

To the CEOs, HR directors and heads of learning and development of these companies, who bravely placed their trust in the processes of experimentation that formed the core of our creative workshops, we owe a special debt of gratitude:

Louise Buckle, Thierry Bonetto, Jacques van den Broek, Emilie Casanova, Priya Chandra-Rogers, Pierre Deheunynck, Pascal Desbourdes, Jade Doyle, Emmanuel Faber, Stephen Frye, Steve Hare, TJ Higgins, Xavier Huillard, Steve Hurst, Isabelle Kocher, Marion Leporcq, Dorothee Lintner, Susie Long, Bruce Lyon, Yusuke Mizukami, Franck Mougin, MC van Niekerk, Patrick Plein, Michelle Prince, Franck Riboud, Nicolas Rolland, Jos Schut, Sikander Sattar and Evelyn van Vosselin.

The challenge that we put to the participants of these management development programmes, held mainly at London Business School, was to design and conduct experiments that would contribute significantly to the performance of the companies for whom they worked. Our role was to guide their endeavours, and the 60-plus examples of business experiments described in the book are just a few of the real-life examples of situations, individuals and teams that we have supported during that time.

The reality, of course, was that we have been learning at least as much from their creativity as they ever did from our instruction. It is almost impossible to recognize so many contributions over a 12-year period and, in the smaller examples, some names or industries have been changed for brevity. In the main case studies and in the appendices, we have been able to describe the businesses more fully and acknowledge those involved in greater detail. To them all we owe an incalculable debt of gratitude – for their forbearance, their enthusiasm and their stunning achievements.

We have also been privileged to be part of a highly diverse and inspirational network of fellow teachers and researchers, with whom we have worked for many years, from whom we have learned abundantly and who have contributed to this book in many ways:

Nana von Bernuth, Julian Birkinshaw, Julie Brennan, Andy Craggs, James Crow, Yves Doz, Francois Dupuy, Tammy Erickson, Giles Ford, Lynda Gratton, Charles Handy, Peter Hinssen, Thomas Hinterseer, Vlatka Hlupic, Dominic Houlder, Richard Hytner, Linda Irwin, Muriel Larvaron, David Lewis, Sir Andrew Likierman, Andrew MacLennan, Costas Markides, John McNelly, Jens Meyer, Nigel Nicholson, Kathleen O'Connor, Tim Orme, Delphine Parmenter, Valerio Pascotto, Chris Rawlinson, Alison Reynolds, Nick Roy, Anil Sachdev, Alan Saunders, Ravi Shankar, Chris Styles, Akin Thomas and Nadya Zhexembayeva.

To Amy Minshull, our commissioning editor at Kogan Page, and Adam Cox, our development editor, we express our profound thanks for their encouragement, advice and companionship.

Finally, we wish to express our love and thanks to Lynne and Gohar.

Introduction

The origins of this book can be found in our work with clients over many years, explaining and guiding them through the experimentation process. We have seen where people get stuck, where they become frustrated, what they find complicated in the process, where caution is required and how obstacles can be overcome. We feel we have probably learned as much from our clients as they might have learned from us. It is why we wanted to capture those insights for the benefit of others.

This book is unusual in its treatment of business experimentation because of its dual approach to the topic. On the one hand, it is a practical guide with downloadable materials that equip the reader with the fundamental tools of experimentation. It allows you to take the process one step at a time at your own pace. It supports you at each stage with activities and templates, while highlighting the pitfalls and how to avoid them.

On the other hand, the book aims to identify aspects of management that are ripe for experimentation. Many workplace practices and processes persist more as a result of habit than efficacy. They urgently demand a more sceptical and experimental treatment. We propose that experimenting with alternative ways of working and bringing the best out of people in an organizational setting is both important and timely.

Synopsis of the book

The book can be viewed as five building blocks that provide the reader with insights at three levels. First, it equips the reader with knowledge of the topic. Second it provides practical guidance for applying that knowledge and, finally, it aims to inspire, enthuse and challenge in equal measure. Our intention is to create a transformative experience for the reader that touches their head, heart and hands.

Setting the scene (Chapters 1 and 2)

The first two chapters provide the foundations for the book. We begin by introducing the reader to the notion that there is a 'spirit' of experimentation – the art of combining curiosity and courage to create breakthroughs. We argue here that corporate performance would be strengthened if there was an improved balance between experimentation and planning. Yet such a shift demands a radical change of mindset if it is to be achieved. The following chapter aims to provide the reader with answers to some of the fundamental questions around business experiments. It provides early insights into what we really mean by experimentation and how it differs from other management practices.

Why experimentation and why now? (Chapters 3 and 4)

In Chapters 3 and 4 we make the case for experimentation in business. We invite the reader to compare traditional methods of management with a more experimental approach to decision-making. We go deeper into defining the characteristics of a good experiment and invite the reader to ponder which aspects of their workplace merit greater examination. Having argued in favour of greater experimentation, we describe how innovation prospers in a crisis but happens much less frequently in 'normal' times. We suggest that the abnormal events of 2020–21 stimulated many businesses to recalibrate their norms and values. There has never been a better time to try out new things and introduce experimentation as an everyday management tool.

The experimentalist (Chapters 5, 6 and 9)

You may work in a global organization or own a small business but, throughout the book, we are conscious that the whole process of experimentation begins with the mindset and attitudes of the individual 'experimentalist'. In Chapter 5 we look at the intrapreneur and the ways in which a single person can influence the wider organization. In Chapter 6 we look at how experimentation is designed to challenge the assumptions that underlie individual behaviours, attitudes and mindsets. We describe them as 'myths' since they are usually so entrenched in daily work practice that they are hardly noticed and rarely questioned. We show that 'normal' business behaviours are often unhelpful or even counterproductive to the development of an experimentation culture. By Chapter 9 the reader will understand more about the required behaviours and also the methodology itself. You will be in a position to reflect on your own preparedness to lead the development of a more experimentally attuned organization. It is here that we provide a self-assessment questionnaire and introduce the 'knowing–doing gap' as a stimulus to take personal action.

Where and how? (Chapters 7 and 8)

In this section we replicate a model that we use in face-to-face sessions by introducing a comparative approach that provides insights from other industries. Our aim is to inspire the reader with ideas and opportunities for experimentation and to show how others have pushed traditional boundaries. We provide several case studies as part of a typology of experiments to illustrate that, even across very different businesses, there are transferable lessons. It is here that we will challenge you to become bolder in your choice of experiments to conduct. Chapter 8 lays out a six-step process of experimentation. In each phase there is an explanation of the rationale and mini case studies to reinforce some of the key messages. It is in this section that we use downloadable guides more extensively as a practical way of following the process alongside the main text.

The experimental organization (Chapters 10, 11 and 12)

The final section of the book focuses on ways in which organizations can develop an experimental culture. We begin in Chapter 10 by reviewing the various dimensions of a corporate culture and explain

how the less visible elements are often the most influential. We identify 10 features that can be found in successful experimental
organizations. They provide a benchmark for assessing your own
organization. In Chapter 11, we invite you to take a pause and step
back. We ask you to consider your own role in nurturing a more
experimental mindset in your organization. Here, we take the view
that a managerial approach is not the best way to dismantle a hierarchical and bureaucratic organization or to build a more experimentally
minded one. As an alternative, we introduce the concepts of 'choice
architecture' and catalytic mechanisms. This leads us to the final
chapter, where we return to the more practical question, 'What can I
do to make this an experimental organization?' Drawing on the
earlier organizational assessment questionnaire, we explain ways in
which you can make a difference in your own organization. It builds
upon the theories and examples introduced in the previous chapter
by providing you with an action plan for becoming a catalyst for
organizational change.

FIGURE 0.1   Building blocks for the experimentalist

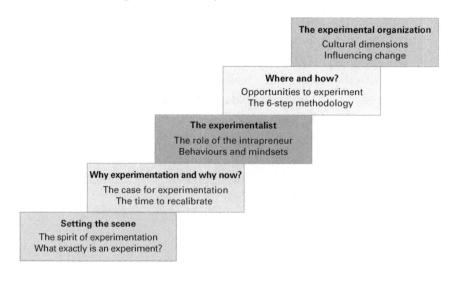

01

The spirit of experimentation

Experimentation is the methodological foundation of the growth of knowledge. It is the surest way of distinguishing between truth and falsehood. By systematizing the process of learning by trial and error, it relies upon the making of mistakes for the making of discoveries. As Richard Feynman, one of the greatest scientists of the 20th century, expressed it:

> If you don't make mistakes, you're doing it wrong.
> If you don't correct those mistakes, you're doing it really wrong.
> If you can't accept that you're mistaken, you're not doing it at all.[1]

Let us start with an example of this process in business.

How productive are you on Wednesday?

In 1930, John Maynard Keynes predicted that, within a century, technological change and rising productivity would cut the average working week to no more than 15 hours, as people chose to increase their leisure time faster than their income.[2]

How wrong he was. The number of hours worked has remained remarkably constant, both in the United States and Europe. Yet Keynes' insight, that rising living standards should lead to more of us deciding that we can meet our material wants and needs through a shorter working week, is causing more of us to ask the question, 'Should we be working four days a week, instead of five?'

Kathryn Blackham, founder and chief executive of Versa, a digital agency based in Melbourne, had long believed that the working week was too rigid. She wondered how best to make it more flexible for her staff. She herself had two young children and was finding her own work/life balance unnatural and out of kilter. She tried various options, such as giving everyone the right to take a number of random days away from the office. But she found that this harmed the collaborative spirit of the firm. So, in 2018, she decided, as an experiment, to close the office from Tuesday evening to Thursday morning. No client meetings. No pressure to answer emails. No pitching for business. In effect, Wednesday joined Saturday and Sunday as fixed days of leisure. She chose Wednesday, and not Friday, for example, because she'd always noticed that Wednesday was 'hump day', with lower levels of creativity and productivity than other days. So, the working week became two intensive 'mini-weeks' separated by a day of 'alternative activity'.

So, what happened? What was the result?

To quote Kathryn, 'We are three times more profitable than we were last year, we have grown by 30 to 40 per cent in the last year in terms of revenue, we have got happier staff and they are much more productive.'

What she discovered was that everyone still worked the same hours each week but with added focus and motivation on the other four days.

Like any discovery, this is counterintuitive. How on earth, by working less does one achieve more, *much more*? Very few corporate executives would have bet on this outcome.

What was Kathryn's genius? Was it that she asked a good question? Or challenged a well-established norm? Or invented a provocative alternative? Perhaps her rarest gift was simply to put into practice her intriguing idea and see what happened. In short, she is that rare being, the business experimentalist. She imagined an alternative way of doing things and had the courage to try it out and be led by the evidence rather than by habit or intuition. After all, many thought leaders have been pondering a shorter working week. But very few have done what Kathryn Blackham has done. This is the lesson of this book.

Experimentation is the art of combining curiosity and courage to create breakthroughs.

The value of experimentation

Everything we know for sure – *or as sure as anything can be* – is the product of experimentation, whether commercial breakthroughs like that at Versa or some of the most sublime discoveries of science.

Think, for example, of the way that gravity bends light,[3] or genes influence behaviour,[4] or brains solve problems.[5] Or, turning from science to technology, consider the safety of a Covid-19 vaccine, a suspension bridge, or a nuclear power station. Or, closer to home, reflect upon the design of the Amazon interface, the Deliveroo supply chain or the Airbnb offer.

Experimentation features less strongly in business than in science. In the chapters that follow, we will be making the case that companies are missing out by not emulating the methods of science. For far too long, business has underestimated the potential of experimentation to enhance performance. Five particular principles explain the value of experimentation to business:

- Experimentation is the surest way we have of distinguishing truths from falsehoods.
- Experiments are the shortest cut we can take to the truth.
- Experiments contribute to our knowledge by turning some of our conjectures into discoveries and some of our convictions into falsehoods.
- Experiments interrogate reality in such a way that nature herself provides the answers to our questions.
- Experimentation, by enhancing our predictive powers, reduces the risks of innovation and makes it economical to be braver in the ideas we test.

In the next chapter, we describe the logic of experimentation in detail, but before doing so, we shall describe two of our own experiments and the lessons they hold for giving experimentation a greater role in business.

Two examples of good business experiments

As London Business School (LBS) tutors, both of us have worked with many of the school's corporate clients over many years to teach experimental design and to supervise the conduct of the ensuing experiments. To give a flavour of the kinds of experiments that are the subject of this book, here, very briefly, are synopses of two such experiments, each conducted by a team of executives from a global pharmaceutical company. Let's see how the principles we describe above play out in practice.

Experiment 1: Why don't we invite outsiders to solve our problems?

A research team, while developing a new drug, had run up against an unexpected problem and they were momentarily at a loss as to how to tackle it. One of the managers closely associated with the research team thought that this problem was a perfect candidate for an LBS experiment. A team gathered around him at LBS and formed an initial hypothesis. 'What if we were to throw the question open to the entire R&D community within the firm and see what advice they might offer?' This would entail sending an email to all 3,800 scientists in the company's R&D labs around the world, specifying the problem and inviting solutions. One member of the experiment team then suggested that they might as well post the same message on the web and see whether anyone not working for the company might have the answer. This suggestion was greeted with laughter. 'Why would someone with no skin in the game take an interest in our problem and spend/devote time coming up with a solution?' But, on reflection, they thought, 'Why not? It's just an experiment. Let's test whether outsiders are cleverer (and more motivated) than our insiders!'

As they went to work on the design of the experiment, they came across an organization, InnoCentive, that specializes in crowdsourcing solutions to technical problems. Headquartered in Waltham, Massachusetts, with an office in London, it has created an open innovation marketplace, in which a network of something like 500,000 experts from across many industries are on tap to help come up with solutions to unsolved problems framed as 'challenges'.

So here we have the germ of an intriguing hypothesis: 'If we communicate our challenge to both our internal scientists and the external crowd, then, with the support of InnoCentive, the most help-ful ideas will come from the crowd.' The experiment corroborated the hypothesis. The crowd not only came up with more ideas but with better ones too, the best of which was a short but powerful monograph on the subject. Problem solved!

This experiment inspired the company to place the same kind of trust in business experiments that they had previously reserved for clinical trials of their drugs and therapies.

Experiment 2: Why don't we get rid of targets for the salesforce?

In another experiment, still with the same company, the issue concerned the incentivization of the salesforce. The prevailing prac-tice within the firm was to set fixed annual sales targets at the beginning of the year. The experiment team had noticed three nega-tive behaviours associated with this practice: first, sales would slacken if targets were reached prematurely; second, sales reps would give up as soon as targets became unachievable; and third, end-of-year sales were overly discounted if targets became 'almost achievable'.

To overcome these negatives, the team imagined replacing the fixed target with a peer-based benchmark. Every sales rep would be encour-aged to 'sell as much as you can' but without a pre-set target. Instead, they would receive a monthly report showing their achievement rela-tive to their peers. The bonus would be based not on their sales relative to target but their sales relative to peer group.

The results were impressive. In Russia, growth of sales in the test group was more than 33 per cent higher than in the control group, with the added benefit of stronger employee engagement; and in Bangladesh, the sales difference was even higher, at 60 per cent. In both countries, 100 per cent of the salesforce voted in favour of the new system.

The eureka factor

These are just two of roughly 150 experiments conducted by this company over the course of 10 years. Many of them took us – and, more importantly, the company itself, including senior management – by surprise. Who could have foreseen with any degree of confidence the outcomes of these experiments? This, of course, is the whole point of experimentation. It has the potential to change minds, and thereby behaviour. It provides the solid evidence needed to rethink the policies, processes and practices of the company, and in so doing re-engineer all three of its management models: the **business model** – how the company competes to create wealth for its customers and shareholders; the **organizational model** – how employees work together to make the most of their collective talents; and its **operating model** – how the company does whatever it chooses to do with the utmost efficiency.

Bringing the eureka factor into your own business

One of the toughest dilemmas facing any company is the balance it strikes between the virtues of planning and control on the one hand and experimentation and learning on the other. The tension between the two arises from a clash of priorities. Plans deal in the values of compliance, alignment and solidarity, whereas experiments are based on the values of speculation, improvisation and playfulness. In Figure 1.1, we portray the dilemma as two feedback loops, each feeding off the company's choice of strategy.

The **planning loop** goes as follows: what do we need to achieve, and by when? (the choice of targets and goals); how will we know we're succeeding? (the choice of metrics and key performance indicators); who deserves what for their achievements? (the choice of incentives and rewards). It assumes that the strategy is a winning strategy, and that therefore its effective implementation is the critical issue that needs careful management.

By contrast the **experimentation loop** is about ideas rather than numbers. The criterion is truth rather than conformity. Its logic runs as follows: to what problems is our strategy the solution? (choice of questions); what alternative strategies could count as better solutions? (formulation of hypotheses); and what evidence would provide the answer? (conduct of experiments). It assumes that the strategy may well be a losing strategy, and that therefore the truth of the

FIGURE 1.1   Rebalancing planning and experimentation

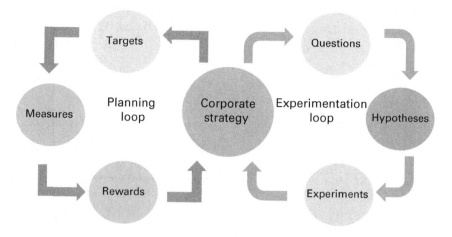

underlying assumptions is the critical issue, if only because a flawed strategy well executed makes things even worse.

Our book is based on three propositions: first, that most organizations devote far more time and effort to the left-hand side of Figure 1.1; second, that corporate performance would be strengthened if more attention were paid to the right-hand side; and third, that it requires a radical change of mindset if the shift in focus is to be achieved.

It is sometimes said that it is better to have questions that can't be answered than answers that can't be questioned. This is a plea for less dogmatism in our thinking and greater curiosity. Experimentation is the best vehicle for expanding our inquisitive imagination.

Summary

Experimentation is a form of adaptive control. It systematizes the logic of trial and error. It uses hard-won empirical feedback to modify beliefs and assumptions. The idea is that behaviours are never left to settle into bad habits, and beliefs are not allowed to become rigid dogma. Nothing is sacrosanct.

In the next chapter, we shift from the **spirit** of experimentation to understand what we really **mean** by experimentation. What is the fundamental process? Where and how can it be used? How does it differ from other management tools?

Notes

1 Richard Feynman (25 August 2020) twitter.com/ProfFeynman/status/1298071162044342272 (archived at https://perma.cc/F3HR-QCN4)

2 Keynes, J M (1931) Economic possibilities for our grandchildren, *Essays in Persuasion*

3 Eddington's 1919 experiment measuring the gravitational deflection of starlight passing near the Sun

4 eg Plomin, R (2018) *Blueprint: How DNA makes us who we are*, Allen Lane, London

5 eg Kahneman, D (2011) *Thinking, Fast and Slow*, Farrar, Straus and Giroux, New York

02

What exactly is an experiment?

In its broadest sense, business experimentation is not new – indeed, it is as old as commerce itself. Merchants and traders over the centuries have explored different ways of attracting new customers, selling more of their products or positioning their services for commercial benefit. The concept of 'trying something out and learning from it' remains as important today as it has ever been, whether it concerns a corner shop trialling a new promotion, an online retailer testing the appeal of different web pages or a global corporation prototyping a new business model.

The logic of the experimental method

Experimentation, which consists essentially of observation under controlled conditions, lies at the heart of the scientific method. It is the most reliable method yet found for discovering – or uncovering – relationships of cause and effect: the idea that changes in one factor (the independent variable) are the cause of changes in another factor (the dependent variable). The skill of experimental design lies in the ability to systematically and precisely manipulate the independent variable(s) while accurately measuring the dependent variable(s). A good experimental design takes account of any third-party influences (extraneous variables) in order to be confident that the observed behaviour of the dependent variable can only be due to the changes in the independent variable.

The difference between experimentation and observation is that an experiment deliberately interferes with reality by administering a particular treatment on a sample of people or process to then observe the response. An observational study leaves reality as it is, and simply notices what is happening. Experimentation, more than observation, tends to be framed in terms of a question to which it seeks answers, or a problem to which it needs solutions. By contrast, observation tends to proceed from the collection of data that is then subjected to analysis in the hope that certain patterns will emerge, and conclusions drawn.

Karl Popper, perhaps the most distinguished philosopher of science of the last century, argued that the injunction, 'observe', makes no sense. We first need a problem or a purpose or a need to orientate our observations and initiate a scientific inquiry. In business, the starting point will often be either a sense of frustration with an existing state of affairs or some playful speculation as to what could or should be an improvement upon it.

The realities of business experimentation

Undoubtedly, business experimentation will play a crucial role as we navigate an increasingly complex business world. There has never been a more compelling case to explore new ways of working than today. But... what exactly is a business experiment, where and how can it be used, what are the benefits, and what is the process?

These are common questions from clients and, while we find there is a general understanding of experimentation, it is clouded by a number of misconceptions. Rarely do we hear people talk about hypotheses, control groups or the more scientific terms of experimentation. Their experience is usually limited to the short, sharp experiments seen in retail environments or where a new process is piloted. Nor do we generally find a clear understanding of how it differs from other business activities such as change initiatives or projects. We observe clients applying the same beliefs and behaviours to experimentation as to other change programmes and then wondering why they are not succeeding.

These are the five areas where misconceptions are most likely to arise:

1 The principles of experimentation: what is its distinctive methodology?

2 The spectrum of experiments: why different opportunities call for different approaches.

3 The role of curiosity: what motivates and inspires effective experimentation?

4 The differences between experiments and projects: what sets them apart?

5 The experiment process: how an experiment is conducted.

1. The principles of experimentation

The following chapters abound with examples of experimentation in its different guises. It is understandable that the question 'what EXACTLY do we mean by experimentation?' arises so frequently when there are so many applications. There *are* different types of experiment and they are described more fully in Appendix A, where you will also find a full glossary of terms.

Most experiments in this book take the form of a comparison. We saw in Chapter 1 how Kathryn Blackham used an experiment to introduce a unique four-day working week for the whole company and compared it with historical evidence. In the example of the Russian sales teams that discarded targets, the comparison was between one group that was exposed to the new arrangements (the experiment or treatment group) and another group that conformed to the existing system (the control group).

In Figure 2.1, we lay out the fundamental elements in any experimental design.

FIGURE 2.1 The elements of experimental design

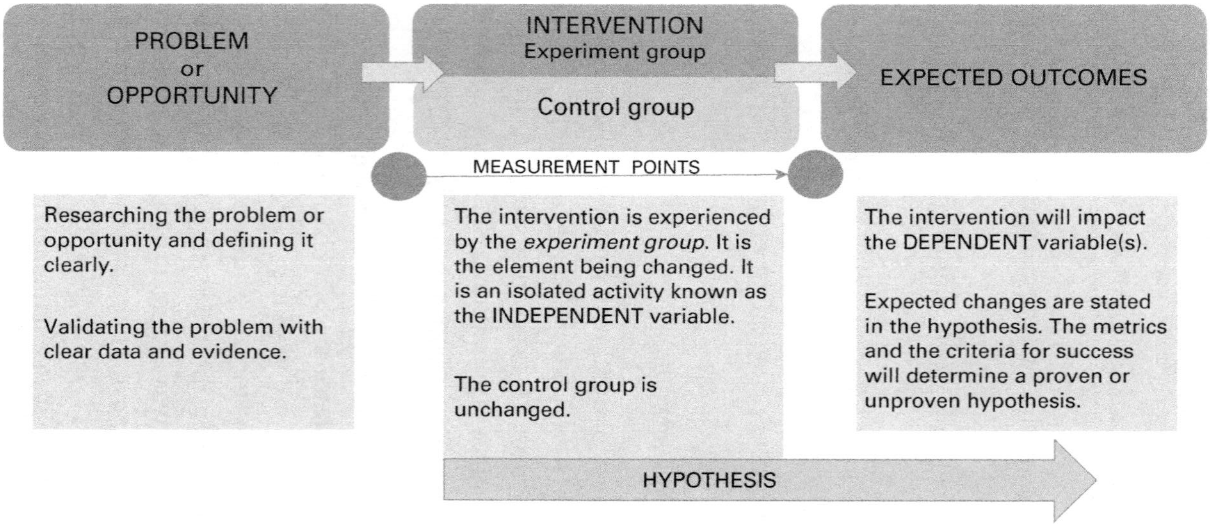

Although illustrated here as a linear process we will see later that experimentation in practice is a highly iterative methodology. In Figure 2.1 we describe how:

- A problem or opportunity is identified and researched to gain a better understanding of the issues.

- A hypothesis is formulated, based on this research, taking the form, 'if action (X) is taken, it will result in outcome (Y)'.

- X is the independent variable and Y is the dependent variable.

- Two groups (A/B) are formed, with the experiment group experiencing the intervention (X) and the control group operating as normal to provide the comparison.

- Baseline measures are taken with both groups at the start of the experiment and again at the end of the experiment.

- Differences between the results of both groups are interpreted as either corroborating or refuting the hypothesis, with a given level of confidence.

- Practical implications are drawn upon and business recommendations made.

Thus, by examining the influence of one variable upon another, while excluding the influence of other variables, a better understanding of the cause–effect relationship is gained. It strengthens the rationality and provides supporting evidence for key decisions to be made by a company and gives greater assurance around those decisions.

2. The spectrum of experiments

People's perceptions of a business experiment are inevitably limited by their personal experiences. In one client organization, experimentation was focused almost entirely on testing minimum viable products (MVPs). In another retail organization, the focus was on short, sharp experiments in product placement. Those involved in each case had little understanding of experimentation in a format different from their own experience. It is why we introduce the concept of a spectrum of experiments that can open people's eyes to a wider variety of approaches to business experiments. Let's illustrate this with a client conversation:

> Jesper is a senior executive in a Nordic financial services organization. An inspirational leader, keen on empowering his teams, he was seeking different ways of improving customer service and increasing revenue. As part of a new initiative, he established small cross-functional teams to come up with ideas for new service offerings. He wanted them to experiment and gave them licence to try out their own ideas. Jesper was rightly proud of his team's efforts, although the results were mixed. In some cases, the findings were fruitful but in others the data was insufficient to draw any clear conclusions. Later, when discussing the rigour of the experimental processes, Jesper remarked, 'But surely this is what experimenting is all about – some you win and some you lose?'

Our response to Jesper's question was 'Yes – and...' Progressive organizations will always be trying out new ways of doing things – new distribution channels, different production processes, alternative ways of working, and so on. This was clearly a positive starting point, with its emphasis on empowering employees and igniting curiosity.

When we discussed the experiments with Jesper, the most successful interventions were the smaller initiatives that possessed a quick feedback loop, resulting in small changes to customer service. In other organizations this might be seen as market testing or piloting. The danger is that people will view this 'try it and see' approach as the endgame of experimentation rather than a creative starting point. Trying something out based on a hunch is fine and definitely has its place, but it hardly differs from the tactics employed by the merchants and traders of past centuries.

In today's competitive environments and in the complex settings of a modern corporation, that type of experiment has limitations. In Jesper's case, the less successful experiments required a more robust, methodical approach to produce data that could be interpreted with greater confidence. That is not to suggest that we should apply a gold standard of techniques that emulate randomized control trials on every occasion.

Business experiments should be seen as part of a spectrum. At one end we have the 'try it and see' approach and, at the other end, more intricate experiments that have the power to influence strategic or operational choices. The higher stakes on the outcomes of the latter demand a much greater 'purity'. That means greater trust in the accuracy of the data and the rigour of the process, enabling business decisions to be made with confidence. The complexity of an experiment and the importance of its outcomes will determine its position on the spectrum and that, in turn, dictates the level of scientific rigour.

However, there will always be trade-offs where it is technically impossible or ruinously expensive to achieve the level of 'purity' necessary. That then becomes a management decision weighing costs against benefits, but it highlights an important point. Business experimentation is first and foremost a management tool, not a fad or theory. It should be seen primarily as a commercial activity supported, where necessary, by a scientific approach that can help business decision-making.

3. The role of curiosity

'We need to be much more creative and innovative as an organization.' 'Our market means we have to be much more agile.' The phrases themselves may change, but the themes are frequent and consistent as we listen to clients discussing experimentation. Companies often see experimentation as a way of promoting innovation and agility within their business and yet, all too often, we see them rewarding managerial practices and behaviours that encourage the opposite. The result is that pockets of the organization may change but, as we describe later, unless structures, systems and attitudes are addressed, there will be little lasting effect.

Experimentation, like curiosity, requires a different mindset. It challenges people and creates discomfort by asking them to adjust entrenched management habits. Chapter 6 describes the adjustments and differences in much more detail, but at this stage we introduce the role of curiosity. The reason is twofold: first, inquiry and curiosity are the bedrocks of the experimental mindset; and second, as you read the next few chapters, we want you to be inspired by the case studies of what others have done. We want you to be curious about how they might relate to your own circumstances. We want to spark ideas that you would like to explore.

We described earlier how experimentation tends to start with a question to which we seek answers, a problem that needs solutions or an opportunity to be explored. With experimentation, you bring an idea, or a theory, or a hypothesis to the table. You have a preconception of what *might* be true, and you're intrigued to discover whether or not it is. It often takes the form, 'What if we were to...?' or 'I wonder if it's true that...?' Only then, in the context of a problem situation, does the experiment start to take shape, and that is why we want you to be curious from the start.

Working recently with one of the 'Big Four' accounting firms, the following were just some of the questions that arose as we began the process. They were framed with an entirely open mind but energized by a burning sense of opportunity and curiosity:

- Let's see if, by devoting 10 per cent of our existing billable hours to in-house innovation projects instead, it would drive up our reputation and success?

- I wonder if we diverted effort from measuring our own performance to measuring the wealth we created for our clients, we would win more repeat business?

- What impact might we have on clients if we swapped jobs with any of our peers for three months on a mutual basis, particularly across business lines? Would this accelerate our learning and serve our clients better?

- What would happen if we were to charge for the wealth that we created for our clients rather than the time we invested in the project?

- If we used crowdsourcing to answer some of our more difficult problems, let's see if we would get more creative, more beneficial solutions.

- Let's explore billing our clients for 90 per cent of the negotiated fee, giving them the option to pay whatever they believed we deserved for the quality of the work delivered.

- What if we have our peers determine our bonuses? It would almost certainly be more motivating and feel more just.

Experimental design is then the art of framing these questions as hypotheses, so as to test which of these is true, and which is false. The experimentation process that we describe in Chapter 8 is the vehicle we use to achieve that.

4. The difference between experiments and projects

Karin is Vice President of Organizational Development in a German-based global chemical company. The company was promoting 'innovation action projects' designed to stimulate new ideas in their six business units. Each project was sponsored by a business unit managing director and each team was given a clear remit and a desired outcome. At an early stage in the initiative, we spoke with Karin about the experimental aspects of the initiatives. In discussing the differences between projects and business experiments, she asked: 'So how much of what we are doing is actually experimenting and how much is project-managing?'

Karin's question is one that we encounter often. While there is certainly a distinction between projects and experiments, it is not always apparent and can contribute to the cloudy perception of what experimentation means. One reason is that project management and change management techniques are an important part of any experiment. A successful experiment requires a robust process to be followed in the same way that a project does. The second reason is that many of the differences are attitudinal. We emphasized earlier that experiments begin with questions in a spirit of curiosity, whereas projects begin with goals in a desire for achievement.

Figure 2.2 sets out the differences in a **purist** version of both projects and experiments. However, categorizing projects and experiments as

FIGURE 2.2   Projects and experiments: a spectrum of characteristics and attitudes

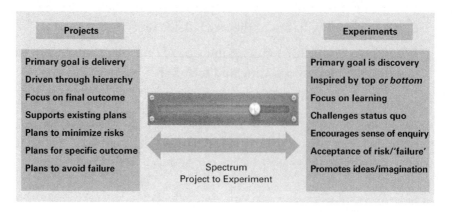

polar opposites is too simplistic. Like experiments themselves, it is better expressed as a **spectrum** of choices that are dependent on the problem or opportunity at hand. For example, in Karin's case, there was a high level of top–down direction in terms of both the content and process, pushing it towards the project end of the spectrum. With Jesper, whose case we considered at the start of the chapter, there was greater empowerment, with ideas and ownership emanating from all levels of the organization. A looser direction in terms of content and process reflected a more experimental approach.

When working with teams we have found it useful to reinforce the use of the term 'experiment' rather than 'project'. It ensures that there is a balance and that the rarer and more precious virtues on the right-hand side are not ignored.

5. The experiment process

We have described in this chapter how business experimentation can be applied in a variety of settings from solving problems and improving performance to influencing strategic choices. We have also high-lighted the demands it places on people to develop different behaviours and mindsets that may be contrary to 'normal' ways of working. Yet, despite the variety of applications across many industries and the variance in management practices, there is one constant: that is the experimentation process itself. We describe each phase in much more detail in Chapter 8, with practical guides and activities, but here we provide an overview as a reference point for the next few chapters.

The process is described in Figure 2.3 as a linear progression, but in reality, it is iterative, with the process going back and forth or overlapping, particularly in the early phases.

We begin with **IDENTIFY**. It is here that curiosity and enquiry drive the process. Topics are proposed, ideas shared, problems discussed and opportunities explored. This stage is about creating options, getting them all out on the table, and not trying to filter or sift them.

As we move to the **DISCOVER** phase, the team is expected to make choices from among the options. They then explore a shortlist of the chosen topics to get 'under the skin' of the problem or opportunity.

This will overlap with the **IDEATE** phase as the team begins to research for possible solutions.

Armed with a shortlist of well-researched topics and ideas, the **DEFINE** phase requires the team to select a single topic and formulate it as a testable hypothesis.

The **EXPERIMENT** phase is how the team proposes to test the hypothesis, including the balance to be struck between the need for scientific rigour and economic value. An experiment might run for several weeks or even months and the time span is dictated by what needs to be measured.

The **EVALUATE** phase is where the team will be collating and analysing the results to propose the recommendations and next steps with the appropriate level of confidence.

Figure 2.3 illustrates the iterative nature of the six-step process.

FIGURE 2.3   A process for experimentation

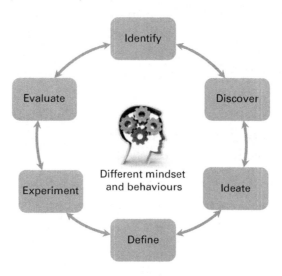

IDENTIFY ➔ Identify the problems, opportunities or gaps you want to address.

DISCOVER ➔ Research and explore the problem or opportunity – internally
and externally.

IDEATE ➔ Widen the scope to seek new ideas for potential solutions and
hypotheses.

DEFINE ➔ Formulate the hypothesis and define the measurability of the
outcomes.

EXPERIMENT ➔ Lay out the practicalities of running the experiment and
testing the hypothesis.

EVALUATE ➔ Analyse and interpret the results. Recommend actions and
next steps.

Summary

We started this chapter by uncovering some of the misconceptions about what is really meant by experimentation. We have described a broad spectrum of experiments and how their level of complexity demands very different approaches. We have highlighted the key characteristics of experiments that remain common even among such varied applications. We have given an overview of a 'typical' process described by the six-step model.

If this chapter has started to answer the 'WHAT?' question, the next chapters will begin to answer the 'WHY?' question. We will be making the case for experimentation and looking more closely at why experimentation should be the chosen tool for managers and why the value of business experimentation has never been timelier than today.

03

The case for experimentation

What is the case for experimentation in business? How do experiments of the kind we have discussed in the last chapter contribute to the performance of a company? In this chapter, we define 10 crucial sources of competitive advantage that accrue to the firm that adopts an experimental mindset. We begin by examining the history of medicine as an exemplar.

The example of medicine

Imagine medicine without experimentation, or pharmacology without clinical trials. In fact, of course, it's easy to do so. For most of history, we relied almost entirely upon quack remedies for the treatment of illness and disease. For example, we had bloodletting, leaches, snake oil, opiates, arsenic, lobotomies, electric shock treatment, mercury, and so on. To some extent, we still do. We have homeopathy, psychoanalysis and many other varieties of 'faith healing'.

The history of medicine is the story, in many cases, of charlatans and magical cures in which those who are sick have chosen – or been encouraged – to place their faith in seemingly effective remedies like McMunn's Elixir of Opium or Dr Kilmer's Swamp Root. It is only within the last century or so that we have relied systematically upon carefully conducted experiments to answer the two fundamental questions raised by any newly formulated treatment, drug or therapy:

- Will it work?
- Is it safe?

These were, after all, the two questions that dominated the concerns surrounding the vaccines as they were developed for the treatment of Covid-19.

Medicine sets a far higher hurdle for its ideas to jump than does business. When we think of progress in medicine, we are thinking essentially of impartial, controlled experimentation. Business prefers to rely essentially upon the competitive market to filter out poor ideas, but this is a very expensive and long-winded way of doing so. Imagine if medicine still had to depend upon the marketplace to determine the difference between what works and doesn't work or what is safe and what is dangerous. Compared with modern medicine, business is remarkably casual about the efficacy of its practices and the veracity of its assumptions. It prefers to rely almost entirely on market signals to judge its performance.

Perhaps companies would place greater faith in their innovative capability if there were faster, more reliable indicators of its quality. When feedback is dilatory and biased, companies prefer to play it safe.

What can management learn from medicine?

In a pioneering experiment in the early 19th century, a physician by the name of Pierre Charles Alexander Louis designed an experiment to show that bloodletting did nothing to cure patients with pneumonia. He found that 44 per cent of those patients who were bled within the first four days of their pneumonia died compared with 25 per cent of those who were bled later in their illness. He inferred that the patients who were treated later were already recovering and that therefore bloodletting made no difference.

In 2020's business, we have econometric forecasting, scenario analysis, strategic market planning and annual budgeting exercises.

We place our faith in behavioural concepts such as authentic leadership, competency profiling, employee empowerment and customer relationship management. How confident are we that they would survive the kind of clinical tests that modern drugs have to pass to be made lawfully available to patients? Is the faith that we place today in hierarchy and bureaucracy any more rational or solid than that which we used to place in bloodletting?

In 2017 Bain & Company's Management Tools and Trends Survey[1] found the 10 practices listed in Table 3.1 to be the most popular. Seventeen years earlier, in 2000, with a few exceptions the picture was rather different.[2]

There would seem to be no rhyme or reason why the popularity of these techniques of management have waxed and waned. Management practice gives the impression of being a product more of fashion and contagion than of evidence and research. By comparison, rational action, as in modern medicine or engineering – and the knowledge that informs it – develops gradually, systematically and cumulatively as the inventive ideas that survive experimentation cohere to form theoretical structures of great power. With management theory, however, there does not seem to be the same path of progress; and this must be due primarily to the lack of experimentation.

TABLE 3.1   Comparison of Bain Management Trends Survey, 2000 vs 2017

2000	2017
1 Strategic planning (76%)	Strategic planning (48%)
2 Mission and vision statements (70%)	Customer relationship management (48%)
3 Benchmarking (69%)	Benchmarking (46%)
4 Outsourcing (63%)	Supply chain management (40%)
5 Customer satisfaction (60%)	Advanced analytics (42%)
6 Growth strategies (55%)	Customer satisfaction (38%)
7 Strategic alliances (53%)	Change Management programmes (34%)
8 Pay-for-performance (52%)	Total quality management (34%)
9 Customer segmentation (51%)	Digital transformation (32%)
10 Core competencies (48%)	Mission and vision statements (32%)

Market competition, of course, is a very powerful selective device. Practices that serve companies well will typically be rewarded and their popularity will grow; but **inside** the company, where competition gives way to compliance and conformity, there are fewer objective tests of the fitness of a company's various tools and techniques.

Another indicator of the sparseness of genuine managerial knowledge is the sheer volume and variety of what is written about it. In science, knowledge becomes expressible in ever fewer words. It has been said that the more we know of any subject, the shorter the book. Darwin's *The Origin of Species* made many, much longer volumes of natural history essentially redundant. Yet, while the book of science is getting shorter, the book of management is getting ever longer. This suggests that very few managerial theories are being refuted. Every idea is given equal worth and weight. There would seem to be no filter – in other words, no experimentation.

The result is that the workplace is ruled as much by superstition as by science. A veritable industry in quack practices has grown up that has enjoyed all the ephemeral properties of a profession, but which, in truth, has no more scientific credentials than bloodletting. Some of these practices will turn out to be effective and wealth-producing, but almost certainly the majority will ultimately be shown to be overblown, injurious or mistaken.

Experimentation – more than a process

In the last chapter we described some of the key elements of an experimental approach – the basic method, the various types of experiment and how they differ from other management practices such as project management. They go some way to answering the question, 'what exactly is an experiment?' but they don't tell us the full story. Experimentation is not simply a process or an activity; it is also an attitude that is less tangible than our earlier technical description.

To explore the question further, let us turn now to the core principles that underpin what we have earlier called the 'spirit of experimentation' that, if practised, bring tangible benefits to the firm. We have grouped them under three broad headings: truth, logic and creativity.

FIGURE 3.1   The principles of experimentation

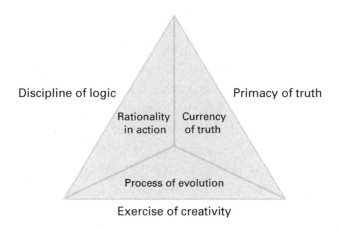

1. The primacy of truth

EXPERIMENTATION DEALS IN THE CURRENCY OF TRUTH

Companies differ profoundly in the answer they give to the fundamental question: 'What – or who – wins arguments in this organization?'
Three answers tend to cover the most important cultural differences
between organizations:

1 For some, it is **power** that wins arguments. Who has the authority
   to make the decision? Who has the right to do so simply by virtue
   of their position in the hierarchy?

2 For others, **expediency** wins out. For example, what are the most
   pressing concerns facing the organization? How are the pressures
   from the markets, or from senior management, forcing certain
   conclusions? The short term often has the strongest voice.

3 The **truth** is what matters most. Of all the assumptions underpinning
   the various options in play, which of them embodies the greatest
   evidential support? Experimental organizations are those that
   assume that if the beliefs that underpin the key decisions of the
   firm are closer to the truth than those of competitors, this is the
   most reliable recipe for corporate success.

An experimental culture is one that places greater weight on truth
than on either power or expediency. It will be one that regards the

pace of organizational learning relative to the competition as the most important measure of corporate performance. In short, it will prioritize knowledge over and above popularity, convenience, the status quo, authority, dogma, productivity, habit or orthodoxy.

At work, there are many values that vie for our attention. We are expected to be efficient. We may want things to be easy, but we nevertheless find the challenge of solving difficult problems deeply satisfying. There is the desire to find life pleasurable and fulfilling. In the company of others, the values of cooperation and collaboration are attractive. And through it all, we seek to be original, creative and highly distinctive. What experimentation honours, however, is the truth.

EXPERIMENTATION COMPENSATES FOR OUR INCOMPETENCE AS PROPHETS

We are not natural futurologists. As humans, we are notoriously bad at predicting the future. It is true that our minds give a lot of thought to what we would do if a certain scenario were to play out; but guessing or anticipating which particular scenario it is likely to be is determinedly not our forte. For example, we are poor predictors of competitive market response. Even armed with market research data and the evidence of focus groups, we're lousy at guessing how consumers will respond to different kinds of product/price offerings.

We're just as hopeless at predicting our own choice of behaviour. Opinion polls have a poor record at predicting the outcome of elections. This may be because we assume that our choices are rational and that therefore we need to look to logical reasons to explain both our own behaviour, and that of others. With the extraordinary success of behavioural economics, we are beginning to understand how our choices are shaped by emotion, context and mental heuristics. Even so, our predictive skills are still not as reliable as the results of a well-conducted experiment.

EXPERIMENTATION ACKNOWLEDGES HUMAN FALLIBILITY

Experimentation starts in the right place – with what we need to know rather than what we need to achieve. It starts with our ignorance, not with our desires. When we start with intention we move quickly to plans, target and milestones, missing the critical ingredients of knowledge, conceptual foundations and competitive differentiation. When we start with ignorance, and an acknowledgment of our own fallibility, we find ourselves exercising curiosity, wondering aloud, listening to each other and forming conjectures. This is the real material out of which genuine strategies are constructed.

Mark Manson puts the argument this way: 'Getting somewhere great in life has less to do with the ability to be right all the time and more to do with the ability to be wrong all the time.' He suggests that the best question that we can ask ourselves is, 'What am I wrong about today that can lead to my improvement?'[3]

EXPERIMENTATION DIMINISHES THE NEED FOR POWER STRUCTURES

Management structures are based on the expensive illusion that humble truth can be replaced by passionate intent, that in business as well as in life we get what we want if we want it strongly enough, and that a powerful sense of purpose can compensate for a flawed strategy. An organization that falls victim to the whims of a narrowly conceived command structure is unlikely to thrive for long.

In 1951, Bertrand Russell formulated a set of commandments that might well stand as a manifesto for a post-hierarchical, experimentally based business.[4] Seven of them are highlighted in the box below.

A MANIFESTO FOR THE EXPERIMENTAL BUSINESS

1 Do not feel absolutely certain of anything.

2 Never try to discourage thinking, for you are sure to succeed.

3 When you meet with opposition, [...] endeavour to overcome it by argument and not by authority, for a victory dependent upon authority is unreal and illusory.

4 Have no respect for the authority of others, for there are always contrary authorities to be found.

5 Do not use power to suppress opinions you think pernicious, for if you do the opinions will suppress you.

6 Do not fear to be eccentric in opinion, for every opinion now accepted was once eccentric.

7 Find more pleasure in intelligent dissent than in passive agreement, for, if you value intelligence as you should, the former implies a deeper agreement than the latter.

2. The discipline of logic

EXPERIMENTATION FORCES US TO MAKE OUR REASONING EXPLICIT

In a typical business plan, how much attention is paid to stating the make-or-break assumptions clearly and simply in a testable format? Or is the plan nothing more than a set of numerical targets? Depending on which it is, what kind of conversation will almost certainly ensue? With assumptions, the debate is likely to hinge on their truth, whereas with targets, the discussion is likely to hinge on their achievability.

In each case, we are relying upon rather different success factors. In the first case, we are counting upon effort, hard work and grit so that even if we badly misunderstand our market, we will still make our goals. In the second case, we are relying upon the truth of our ideas such that even if they are poorly implemented, we will still succeed. Ultimately, is business a test of perspiration and perseverance or inspiration and insight? In the long run, which of these mindsets is more likely to win?

The experimental frame of mind says: stop asking, 'what results do you want to achieve, what outcomes would count as success, and what numbers do you need to make?' These are banal questions to which every competitor in an industry will have broadly similar answers. Start asking instead: 'what assumptions are you banking on to deliver these outcomes, and what evidence do you have that they are true?'

Antoine de St Exupéry declared that, 'What separates us is not our aims – they all come to the same thing – but our methods, which are the fruit of our varied reasoning.'[5] For too long, companies have relied upon the choice of objectives to differentiate their market offer and guide their behaviour, as opposed to the quality of the ideas that underpin their strategies.

EXPERIMENTATION DIRECTLY ADDRESSES MANY OF THE CORPORATE NEUROSES OF OUR TIME

The prevailing pathology in companies may, with poetic licence, be described as follows:

- defensiveness: 'play safe', 'stay in control';
- loss aversion: 'be careful', 'make no mistakes';

- catastrophizing: 'dream vaguely, dread precisely';
- delay: 'wait till we know for sure', 'kick the can down the road';
- uncertainty: 'treat it as a threat, not an opportunity';
- doorknob polishing: 'be efficient', 'stick to the knitting', 'cut costs';
- rain-dancing: 'prepare a plan';
- illusion of certainty: 'build a budget';
- plagiarism: 'adopt best practice';
- bossism: 'toe the line';
- learned helplessness: 'I can't, I won't, I daren't';
- right first time: 'wrong for ever'.

Experimentation gives us the tools to determine whether or not these habits of thought are productive or not.

3. The exercise of creativity

EXPERIMENTATION EMULATES THE PROCESS OF EVOLUTION

The logic of evolution is one of variation followed by selection. The most important element of this logic is that the fitness that it creates does not depend on any mechanism of design. In this sense, evolution is blind. The mutations that survive long enough to reproduce are not the outcome of a purposeful process. They are, in this sense, random. What looks like progress is a function purely of the selective mechanism of survival. Thousands of seemingly random mutations are cast into the 'lottery' of survival and reproduction and only then does the rigorous process of selection begin.

In science, of course, an immense amount of thought and imagination goes into the construction of hypotheses. But the important point is that this is not always a necessary component of scientific discovery. Many scientific breakthroughs have resulted from the testing of quasi-random or accidental theories. And in business the value of experimentation is that it sifts thousands of half-baked, idiosyncratic ideas into buckets labelled true and false, or effective and ineffective, or wealth-productive and wealth-destructive.

The idea of 'right first time' is as nonsensical in business as it would be in science or the biology of evolution. 'Wrong first time' would make for a much better motto. It has been well observed that if evolution had relied upon total quality management, lean principles and top–down planning, we would still be amoeba.

Matt Ridley, in his celebrated book *The Evolution of Everything*, has suggested that:

> If there is one dominant myth about the world, one huge mistake we
> all make, one blind spot, it is that we all go around assuming the world
> is much more of a planned place than it is... change in technology,
> language, mortality and society is incremental, inexorable, gradual and
> spontaneous... much of the human world is the result of human action,
> but not of human design... it emerges from the interactions of millions,
> not from the plans of a few.[6]

EXPERIMENTATION LIBERATES THE HUMAN IMAGINATION

Experimentation gives licence to the wilder forms of imagination. The importance of this lies in the recognition that great entrepreneurial ideas are rarely self-evident. They contain an eccentric or idiosyncratic element. We need to stray outside our notions of common sense if we are to bump into great business ideas.

Experimentation has the effect not only of inspiring people to be more imaginative in the options worth considering, but also more disciplined in the evaluation of these options. This contrasts sharply with the standard method of strategizing, in which very little creativity goes into the **content** of the strategy, whereas a spirit of 'anything goes' is invested in its **execution**, just so long as the targets are met.

Experimentation encourages boldness of conjecture by ensuring that any test is conducted on only a small part of the organization. By not 'betting the farm', it encourages employees to test a much greater span of ideas than would be the case if the costs of failure were born by the business as a whole.

In effect, experimentation trades efficiency for truth. It plays with a multitude of possible ideas, rejecting most of them, just to get to a single proposition that is not only true, but unique to the firm. Its great virtue is that it is the cheapest and surest way of getting from lots of wild ideas to one or two genuine discoveries. The effort goes not so much on the design of the idea (the strategy) as on the rigour of the experimental filter (the testing process). Business, like life and science, can be managed and treated as a numbers game.

EXPERIMENTATION FOCUSES ON THOSE QUESTIONS TO WHICH ANSWERS ARE MOST NEEDED

The hardest part of experimentation is to identify a problem whose solution would contribute to the performance of the firm. 'What don't we know that we need to know?' In business, identifying the area of ignorance within which untapped wealth resides is difficult. We are all familiar with the ease with which management teams can fill flipcharts with lists of problems, but they are rarely stated in such a way as to lead to innovative, wealth-creating solutions. They tend to be bland and generic: 'How can we increase sales? How can we differentiate our product?' A good question resembles a design brief that has the capacity to inspire a creative solution.

This is the challenge, for example, that the Citroen executive board put to its engineers in the late 1930s:

> A car that can carry four farmers and over 100 pounds of their
> harvested crops to market over unpaved roads… managing 80 miles per
> gallon while doing so… and making sure that the car can drive across
> a ploughed field loaded up with eggs and not breaking them… and also
> able to carry awkward goods like furniture….

The result was the Citroen 2CV, launched in 1948 and manufactured until 1990. Thirty years later, in 2020, an equally eccentric car, the Citroen Ami, was launched to great acclaim. It aimed to emulate the practicality and iconic success of the 2CV. This was the question to which it was the answer:

> How can we provide easier access to city centres, micromobility for
> everyone, and a genuine alternative to scooters, bicycles, mopeds and
> public transport – all at an affordable price?

The result was the Ami, a light quadricycle less than five feet wide and eight feet long. It seats two people. It is powered by a 6kW motor and a 5.5kWh battery. Its top speed is 28mph, with a range of 47 miles. It has been described as an 'urban mobility object' priced to compete with public transport. You don't need a driving licence, so in theory, a 16-year-old can drive it in Paris.

Experimentation needs well-crafted questions if it is to get to imaginative solutions.

EXPERIMENTATION IS THE PURSUIT OF UNCOMMON SENSE

The experimental mindset is one that relishes creativity and the playful invention of possible truths. It is not afraid of appearing naïve or foolish or unorthodox. It's not unsettled or unnerved by setbacks, false trails or experimental glitches. It recognizes that for an idea to qualify as a solution to a genuine problem, it will probably seem at first sight to be absurd, nonsensical or bizarre. If it were sensible, it would already have been widely adopted. It knows that the act of experimentation quickly and cheaply rejects those that genuinely don't make sense. But it also recognizes that many problems in business do not get solved if only because the solutions are drawn from too orthodox a mindset. They are too 'safe', too 'sensible' or too 'sanguine'.

'Right first time' has been a particularly harmful philosophy of business. It took James Dyson 15 years and 5,127 prototypes to create the bag-free, cyclone-technology vacuum cleaner. 'Prototype' is the scientific word for 'error'. In the pursuit of progress there can be no shortcut. We are condemned to having to gather the evidence of an idea's worth only **after** we have had the idea. There is no direct route from observation to discovery.

Provocation

In our seminars with clients, when these arguments are being made, there is invariably one manager at least who suggests that therefore they should have the right to conduct experiments on behalf of the organization. Our response is that this should be regarded not only as a right but also as a duty. None of us goes to work to make happen what is going to happen anyway. We go to work to make a difference. Experimentation should be the principal method by which we do so.

Notes

1   Rigby, D and Bilodeau, B (5 April 2018) Management tools and trends: 5 key trends emerged from Bain's survey of 1,268 managers, www.bain.com/insights/management-tools-and-trends-2017/ (archived at https://perma.cc/ED8N-RTVD)

2   Ibid

3   Manson, M (2020) Why I'm wrong about everything (and so are you), markmanson.net/wrong-about-everything (archived at https://perma.cc/NZ5Z-UXSZ)

4   Russell, B (16 December 1951) The best answer to fanaticism – liberalism, *New York Times Magazine*

5   De Saint-Exupéry, A (1939) *Wind, Sand and Stars*, Harcourt Brace, New York

6   Ridley, M (2016) *The Evolution of Everything: How new ideas emerge*, Harper Perennial, London

04

Now is the time

In the spirit of never letting a good crisis go to waste, what have we learned about management and the workplace from the way that the world reacted to the Covid-19 pandemic of 2020? In this chapter, we explore two concrete lessons to have come out of the crisis that could accelerate organizational learning.

Tom Peters, a management guru, wrote during the pandemic: 'This is a once-in-a-lifetime opportunity to enact positive change and plant the seeds for a better world... don't blow it.'[1] And Klaus Schwab, founder and executive chairman of the World Economic Forum, observed: 'The pandemic represents a rare but narrow window of opportunity to reflect, re-imagine, and reset our world.'[2]

If we are to reset the world of business, there are two invaluable lessons that can be taken from the corporate response to the pandemic:

1 Companies habitually **underinvest** in experimentation.
2 Organizations **overrate** their traditional ways of working.

Both these forms of irrationality have long acted as obstacles to wealth-creation and corporate performance.

Underinvesting in experimentation

Experiencing the pandemic and responding to the problems that it posed have been the ultimate natural experiment. It has, in effect, thrown into doubt many of our most cherished social and economic assumptions and put to the test many of our everyday practices.

The lessons of locking down whole economies have been many and varied, but perhaps the most important has been that we learn more boldly and more assuredly from an experimental attitude to reality than from any other. It has taught us that, when forced to lead an experimental life – when we resort to trial and error – we are at our best, in so far as we learn faster and better than we do in normal times or when left to create our own experimental agenda.

Experimentation, for all its sound and fury, throws up remarkable insights and breakthroughs. We come to see each other and our institutions – as well as ourselves – in a new light. Who would have guessed how resourceful we have been? Thousands of companies 'rolled up their sleeves', threw away the rulebook and repurposed their facilities to meet the pressing needs of health services around the world and to help wherever and however they could.

Rory Sutherland, vice chairman of Ogilvy, made the following, insightful observation:

> The newspapers are full of stories about how small groups of engineers from Formula 1 teams like McLaren have been able to design, prototype and manufacture essential health equipment incredibly quickly. So why aren't organizations allowed to perform such super-human feats of brilliance the rest of the time?[3]

McLaren, a UK-based Formula 1 constructor, was not alone:

- In Spain, Acciona used 3D printers to manufacture protective masks.
- In Germany, Siemens produced 50 million antibody tests per month.
- In the US and Canada, Hewlett-Packard provided connectivity kits to healthcare facilities.
- In China, JD.com deployed drones to conduct ground surveys, design flight corridors and conduct flight tests to deliver essential goods to fight the pandemic.

- Volkswagen provided German hospitals and nursing homes with breathing masks, thermometers, disinfectant, protective goggles and suits... as well as 3D printing mountings for face shields.

- In India, the Mahindra Group developed low-cost respirators.

- In the UK, Rolls-Royce and Ford joined forces to deliver 10,000 ventilators to the NHS.

- Mastercard and Wellcome, with the Bill and Melinda Gates Foundation, launched a Covid-19 Therapeutics Accelerator.

- LEGO® focused on children's access to learning through play during lockdown.

... and so on, and so on.

The world surprised itself by the energy, goodwill and can-do attitude that it brought to the situation. Covid-19 tapped into the best in human nature. It showed that, in a crisis, humankind turns naturally, instinctively and skilfully to experimentation and the prototyping of potential solutions. When there is no answer to hand, we use trial and error as the surest method of finding fast and ingenious solutions.

Lockdown brought out two hugely undervalued human talents – curiosity and improvisation. It showed that business is at its best when facing a challenge rather than delivering a plan or meeting a target. We drain business of its natural zest when we assume that work is a penance and that people need incentivizing if they are to give of their best. We so often misjudge what motivates people and underestimate their latent energy. In general, people are overmanaged and underchallenged. Perhaps leadership is essentially the art of creating these experimental conditions that draw upon natural human talent. Let us hope that the hard-won lessons of the pandemic are not lost in a post-pandemic world. This recalls the maxim of W Edwards Deming's, the inventor of total quality management: 'We must preserve the power of intrinsic motivation, dignity, cooperation, curiosity, joy in learning, that people are born with.'[4]

Overrating conventional work habits

The crisis reminded us, if we ever needed reminding, that we are fallible beings. Working from home (WFH) has led to unexpected outcomes, extraordinary discoveries and a taste for greater experimentation. We found that many of our workplace assumptions, based on a rather cynical view of human nature, were flawed.

The experience caused us to ask an unfamiliar range of questions: 'What if we all had to work from home?' 'What if we were each trusted to manage our own work, unsupervised?' 'What if the only or the main vehicle of communication and coordination was virtual meetings?' 'What if each of us set our own work agenda?' 'What if we chose our own pace and hours of work?' 'What if face-to-face meetings were set aside in favour of remote working?'

What was revealed was the sheer resourcefulness, self-management skills and goodwill of the vast majority of employees, accompanied by a corresponding sense of liberation, responsibility and fulfilment. In many cases, people were more productive, more creative and more fulfilled working from home than in the office. Work would seem to have become more purposeful and meaningful.

The experience also highlighted three aspects of office life that have been shown by this natural experiment to be mistaken:

1 The conceit that most people are untrustworthy, disorderly or feckless and that therefore they need a boss to organize and structure their work on their behalf.

2 The tacit assumption that the future is most reliably realized if it is made to look and feel like a jigsaw puzzle, entirely pre-planned down to the last piece, and that there is a right way to assemble the pieces.

3 The premise that a five-day work week, clocking in and out, being visible to our colleagues, and working together physically are intrinsic to productive work. The waste inflicted upon the organization by these beliefs has been estimated at 35 per cent.[5]

We would never have tried out these new ways of working or made these discoveries if we hadn't been compelled to. One wonders what other truths are waiting to be uncovered simply because we haven't had sufficiently pressing reasons to be so inventive. What else do we take for granted that 'just ain't so', to quote a saying attributed to Mark Twain?[6]

If we take modern marketing practice as an example, many traditional assumptions about how consumers choose brands have had to be radically revised in the light of empirical studies of brand choice behaviour originating with ASC Ehrenberg and pursued further by Byron Sharp and his colleagues.[7] These are just a few of the widely held misconceptions that have been overturned by experimentation and analysis:

- A brand's customers are demographically and psychologically distinct from those of its direct competitors (**market segmentation**).
- A brand's competitors are determined by the claims and appeals that it makes (**brand positioning**).
- A brand's heaviest 20 per cent of customers deliver more than 80 per cent of its sales (**the 80/20 rule**).
- A brand's sales growth comes more efficiently from reducing the defection of its buyers than acquiring new buyers (**brand loyalty**).

Since its origins, microeconomic theory too has fallen victim to untested theories, such as the assumption that consumers compare brands on the basis of their utility, that they are not influenced by the behaviour of other consumers, that context and emotion play no part in decision-making, and that past behaviour makes no difference. Underlying these beliefs was the conviction that human beings are able to describe accurately the process by which they come to a decision and make a choice. Only when behavioural scientists such as Amos Tversky and Daniel Kahneman started to test these beliefs were they shown to be mistaken.

Experimentation derives its potency from the fact that so many of the theories that we take for granted are false, and costly.

We are problem-solving creatures

'All life is problem-solving,' as Karl Popper expressed it.[8] The examples we quoted earlier of how companies responded to the pandemic demonstrate that we are at our best, in terms of both energy and imagination, when solving urgent and important problems rather than, say, achieving arbitrarily set goals or applying formulaic solutions. The experimentally attuned organization is one that taps into this spirit of 'applied curiosity' to manage, not just periodic crises, but also everyday business.

There are two crucial components of an experimental culture that upset the standard way of doing business:

- Managers act their way into new ways of thinking, rather than think their way into new ways of behaving.
- Managers rely more upon serendipity – the luck of bumping into brilliant solutions – than upon foresight.

Let us take each in turn.

Acting our way into new ways of thinking

The nature of business is that each day brings opportunities disguised as problems. We're easily tempted to ponder these problems – sometimes for months on end – in the belief that, with time, the opportunity will reveal itself and the solution will become clear. By contrast, the experimental mindset prefers to take action. It assumes that the results of these actions – whether positive or negative – will provide us with more information than any amount of reflection.

The fact is that, without action, nothing ever gets achieved. Without trials, there are neither errors nor breakthroughs. What is more, we often find that by trying out a plethora of tentative solutions, we get a better fix on the problem. We see the issue for what it is and this gives us stronger indications as to where the solution lies. We are encouraged to keep acting. We get to the solution by making our mistakes faster than we would otherwise. In a sense, business is a numbers game, and we need sufficient numbers of trials for serendipity to work in our favour. Waiting for 'the right idea' to come to us, or 'the right moment' to act, is a form of collective neurosis, disguising our fear of failure.

One is reminded of Churchill's famous dictum, 'action this day'. His policy in the Second World War was to put every problem into one of two buckets: either 'action this day' or 'report in three days'. In both cases, there were things to be done. But whatever the challenge, he insisted on **some** action being taken **every** day if progress were to be made.

To summarize, there are two methods of making progress:

1 **Thinking more** so as to act more **logically.**

2 **Acting more** so as to think more **realistically.**

The experimental mindset is wedded to the second. It defines the object of business as **opportunities** to be seized rather than **plans** to be achieved. Particularly in 2020's world of disruption and unpredictability, our traditional reliance on plans and budgets rather than experimentation and agility would seem to be misplaced.

Relying more upon luck than foresight

> If you believe success is mostly due to luck, there are strategies you can pursue to lure luck out of hiding. By contrast, if you believe that orderly plans, and getting up an hour earlier than the next person are the answer, then by all means arise before the rooster and start planning.[9]

This is how Tom Peters interpreted the management of luck. He believed that luck, defined as 'a chance happening of fortunate or adverse events', could be turned to one's advantage. Rather than wait for chance events to happen, the experimental mindset is one that purposefully sets out to create events that throw up the kinds of chance happenings from which we can learn.

Among the strategies that Peters recommended for 'getting lucky', here are his top three:

· More times at the plate, more hits.

· Try it. Cut the baloney and get on with something.

· Ready. Fire. Aim. (Rather than Ready. Aim. Aim. Aim...)

Serendipity is the faculty of making fortunate discoveries by accident. It has played a significant role in scientific discovery and business innovation. We can leverage serendipity by adopting an experimental mindset. Through greater use of trial and error, what looks like an accidental discovery can become more like an inevitable breakthrough. In this sense, fortune favours the profligate: a tolerant attitude towards large numbers of errors turns a process of accidental discovery into one of systematic organizational learning.

Serendipity accepts that what is found is not necessarily what was being looked for. This is a version of the oblique principle, the idea that we don't get what we aim for and that therefore our goals are best achieved indirectly. In the history of science, for example, many experiments made lucky discoveries while investigating other things. This kind of luck is more likely to favour the management team that acts serendipitously rather than thinking strategically.

A striking case of serendipity during the testing of Covid-19 vaccines was the 'accidental' discovery by the Oxford/AstraZeneca team that, if the first shot contained only half a dose, it was significantly more effective.

Two contrasting approaches to corporate success

For most companies, strategy is a single big bet. It is invented and formulated by quite a small team of senior executives. The view is that they are in the best position to see the future and create a winning formula. It is for the rest of the organization to implement it. There are, in effect, a small number of thinkers and a large number of doers. Implementation becomes the performance-defining issue, and when things go wrong it is assumed to lie in clumsy execution rather than misconceived strategy. Thus, the dominant values of the organization will tend to be those of loyalty, alignment and solidarity. They reflect a managerial mentality grounded in habits of centralization, control and compliance. Yet it remains the case that 'betting the farm' on an untested bold conjecture is a huge gamble.

In contrast to the single big bet, 'planned serendipity' can be seen in the dramatic success of the 'marginal gains' methodology made famous by the Tour de France victories of Team Sky, coached by Sir Dave Brailsford. Applied to business, this is a technique of thinking that focuses on incremental changes to everything in the organization, 1 per cent at a time. Unlike the big bet strategy, it relies upon the compounding effect of multiple small wins. Improving the firm by 1 per cent every day means ending the year 37 times better! It is a form of piecemeal engineering. In earlier times, it was called evolutionary operation (EVOP), emulating the variation and selection method of Darwinian theory.

Of the hundreds of experiments that led to British cyclists winning 178 world championships and 66 Olympic or Paralympic gold medals between 2007 and 2017, here are just a handful:

- Tyres gained grip by being coated with alcohol.
- Racing suits were tested in wind tunnels to become more aerodynamic.
- Workouts were enhanced through biofeedback sensors.
- Muscle recovery was accelerated by certain massage gels.
- A good night's sleep was improved by particular pillows and mattresses.
- Muscle temperature was optimized by wearing electrically heated overshorts.
- Finely tuned bikes were degraded even by small amounts of dust in the team truck.

Marginal gains such as these should serve as an inspiration to any organization that aspires to excel. Strategy for the experimental company is managed as an emergent process – more like a shower of arrows fired into the future than a preconceived plan being remorselessly rolled out.

Four styles of experiment

Experiments can be big, 'bet the farm' type experiments: the entire company becomes the hypothesis and therefore, by definition, they are a rare occurrence for the firm adopting such an experiment. Equally, experiments can be small, 'farm the bets' type experiments: each experiment is contained within a small part of the company and therefore many experiments can be running concurrently.

Every new business is self-evidently a single bet. It is testing one big idea. But as the business grows, and as it becomes multi-divisional, the opportunity for multiple experimentation expands. Most of the examples in this book are experiments conducted synchronously within different parts of the same organization. This is what we mean by an experimental culture. In some organizations, such as booking. com and Amazon, hundreds, if not thousands, of fast-paced, tightly designed experiments are running in parallel. This style of experimentation lies at the heart of what has been called the 'learning organization'. It contrasts sharply with the organization that still relies solely upon a yearly strategic planning process to place its bets and steer its course.

In Figure 4.1, we depict the space within which different approaches to experimentation can be mapped.

FIGURE 4.1   The scale and pace of experimentation

Summary

The pandemic has whetted the appetite for experimentation. It has encouraged business to place the emphasis on organizational learning rather than operational efficiency. Punit Renjen, Global CEO of Deloitte, expressed the challenge in this way: 'The crisis can become an opportunity for companies to create even more value and positive social impact, rather than just bounce back to the status quo.'[10] This is the ideal moment to develop a corporate culture of greater experimentation. It also challenges individual managers to invent new ways of working and to explore the full potential of experimentation.

In the next two chapters we look at the dual roles of the intrapreneur and the entrepreneur: how the individual can make a difference and what skills are needed.

Notes

1 Peters, T (June 2020) *Now More Than Ever*, Tom Peters Times, www.zdnet. com/article/tom-peters-an-excellent-legacy-of-extreme-humanism/ (archived at https://perma.cc/V7NN-6FBB)

2 Schwab, K (3 June 2020) Now is the time for a 'great reset', www.weforum. org/agenda/2020/06/now-is-the-time-for-a-great-reset/ (archived at https:// perma.cc/AR4H-MXMV)

3 Sutherland, R (25 April 2020) What bees can teach us about efficiency, *Spectator*, www.spectator.co.uk/article/what-bees-can-teach-us-about-efficiency (archived at https://perma.cc/ZA3K-76JE)

4 Edwards Deming, W (1994) *The New Economics for Industry, Government, Education*, MIT Press, Boston

5 Workforce Institute (4 September 2018) The case for a 4-day workweek?, workforceinstitute.org/the-case-for-a-4-day-workweek-nearly-half-of-employees-worldwide-could-do-their-jobs-in-5-hours-or-less-each-day/ (archived at https://perma.cc/VB4R-JF59)

6 At London Business School, for example, more progress was made during 2020 on the art and skill of virtual teaching than throughout the preceding decade.

7 Sharp, B (2010) *How Brands Grow: What marketers don't know*, Oxford University Press, Oxford

8 Popper, K (1999) *All Life is Problem-solving*, Routledge, Abingdon

9 Peters, T (March 2021) The pursuit of luck, tompeters.com/columns/
the-pursuit-of-luck/ (archived at https://perma.cc/6DPA-6KJG)

10 Sidorovich, Y (February 2021) Leadership in the crucible of crisis, Deloitte,
www2.deloitte.com/si/en/pages/about-deloitte/articles/the-heart-of-resilient-
leadership.html (archived at https://perma.cc/5G4D-R7GN)

05

The experimentalist: Intrapreneurs and entrepreneurs

The experiments featured in this book almost always involve groups or teams. In some cases, the teams were appointed or self-selected as part of a leadership development programme. In other situations, they were intact teams exploring experimentation as a new way of working or as an organizational initiative. In both cases there is a collective approach to experimentation where ideas, decisions and responsibilities are shared and there is a support structure to guide the process. Most of our work in the last 12 years has been in group settings, but at a seminar a few years ago we were reminded how easy it is to overlook the *individual* aspects of experimentation. Naturally, organizations play an important role in creating the *environment* for innovators to flourish (or not!). However, organizations do not innovate; the people within them do. Organizations are not creative; the people within them are. Organizations do not change; their people do.

It is the *individual* that becomes our focus in the next two chapters. We look at the challenges and opportunities through the eyes of two types of innovator – the aspiring experimentalist (**the intrapreneur**) and the small business owner (**the entrepreneur**).

Intrapreneurship – the time is right

Satoshi is a VP in a US-based hotel chain. He was attending the seminar as an individual participant. He listened intently to the discussions of the other 30 candidates, who were mostly in small teams of 5 or 6. Most of them had already started to embrace experimentation as a way of working. They were there to gain further insights. Satoshi spoke to us during a break: 'I'm fascinated and inspired by all the stories I'm hearing. I've a load of ideas of my own but my own organization is not sponsoring these types of initiatives. I'm part of a management team but I'm finding it difficult to see where and how I can start or even prepare to start.'

There will be many readers of this book, like Satoshi, whom we would describe as an 'intrapreneur' or an organizational 'pioneer'. They are often a lone voice, sometimes frustrated by the systems and processes around them and wanting to make work more meaningful. They have an entrepreneurial mindset that feels constrained by an organizational ecosystem.

There are plenty of examples of this type of intrapreneur creating products or services that have transformed their organizations, but it is rarely an easy task. The headlines usually focus upon the story of a bright and creative employee hatching a big idea. However, the real story is more to be one of getting an organization that shuns risk and adheres to traditional management practices to take notice.

Ken Kutaragi was a junior employee at Sony who spent hours tinkering with his daughter's Nintendo to create a more powerful, user-friendly game. His idea was continually rebuffed by Sony bosses, hesitant to join the gaming industry, until one senior manager thought the idea was worth a try. PlayStation was launched only to become the best-selling games console today.

The Post-It note is regularly lauded as an example of an intrapreneurial success story. It was in 1968 that Spencer Silver and Art Fry at 3M discovered how a weak, pressure-sensitive adhesive could have a variety of uses. Their bosses, understandably, couldn't see the value in an adhesive that would hardly stick! It took a further nine years to gain management acceptance that resulted in an experiment in four cities. The experiment was considered to have 'failed' since nobody bought the product – but it was not a 'failure' in an experimental sense. It provided valuable customer insights. A year later the experiment was repeated, and the rest is history.

When Eric Favre had his first idea for Nespresso pods and machines after watching baristas in Rome, he didn't envisage his idea taking so long to reach the marketplace. With a patent granted in 1976 and an enthusiastic partner in Jean-Paul Gaillard to commercialize the product, it still took a further 10 years for the product to launch. The inertia was a result of Nestlé's fears that it would be competing against its own products, such as their instant coffee, and that an 'exclusive' brand approach simply didn't suit an FMCG company. Even after launch, there were many production and styling problems to overcome before it attained today's position where 14 billion Nespresso capsules are sold every year, both online and from 810 brightly lit boutiques in 84 countries.

The examples above show how an intrapreneur can make a huge difference to a business but that it is rarely an easy ride and that it takes a lot more than an idea. In each of the Nespresso, 3M and Sony examples, the organization finally took note. In other cases, the outcome is not always as positive.

At Eastman Kodak in 1973, a 24-year-old Steve Sasson was working on a project that, in his words, 'was just a project to keep me from getting into trouble doing something else'. His project resulted in an idea for an all-electronic camera that didn't use film. Neither did it use paper or any consumables in capturing and displaying photographs. It was the first digital camera. Sasson's job was even harder than that of Silver, Fry and Kutaragi because it was not simply the organizational inertia he was facing. The digital camera was a direct threat to the Kodak business model, which relied upon the sales of film and paper consumables. Kodak owned the patent for Sasson's idea until 2007, but the company never truly embraced digital technology. Sasson's original camera is now in the Smithsonian Museum. He was awarded a national medal for technology and innovation in 2009. Kodak filed for bankruptcy in 2012.

The three stories show that the role of the intrapreneur or the individual experimentalist is never going to be an easy one. Despite that, we feel that there has never been a better time than now for intrapreneurs to flourish. Almost all the conversations we have with client organizations include aspirations to be more innovative and agile as they face an increasingly complex business world. There appears to be a genuine desire among leaders, in even the most traditional organizations, to make changes. They are learning the lessons of the examples above and seeing ways in which more progressive organizations are embracing intrapreneurial ideas to create competitive advantage.

Amazon programmer Peri Hartman's idea of a 'buy with one click' button was patented by the organization in 1997. It licensed the technology to others, such as Apple iTunes, and by the time the patent expired in 2017, Amazon's turnover was $177 billion.

Mary Cobb's idea of humorous ad libs for Southwest Airlines safety briefings became a YouTube hit. Eagerly adopted by senior management, it soon became a feature of all of their flights and has been estimated to be worth £140 million a year in increased customer loyalty.

Companies that have ridden the technology wave of the 21st century, like Intel, Shutterstock and DreamWorks, embrace initiatives that encourage employee creativity as a central part of their business. Others, like Google and W.L. Gore, provide dedicated time for employees to work on 'personal projects' as part of their job. The 'traditional' organizations have been taking note and following their example. That is not to suggest that the experimentalist and the intrapreneur will be welcomed with open arms. Not every organization is willing to experiment like Google or Intel, but there is an increasing acceptance in business that the intrapreneur can play a crucial role.

If the tide had already started to turn in favour of the intrapreneur, the post-pandemic era has seen an acceleration of the changes. The need for businesses to recalibrate has never been greater. More than ever before, organizations are examining their business models and experimenting with how they deliver services and organize work.

Our conversations with Satoshi, along with the increased opportunities for others like him, prompted us to prepare a set of guidelines for the intrapreneur. They are written for the individual 'experimentalist', for the lone voices striving to create a more innovative approach to the way business is done. The focus is on the individual, but we begin with the organization.

How ready is your organization?

Intrapreneurs can sometimes be fooled by the rhetoric they hear from the organization. Take any number of large organizational websites and try to find one that doesn't mention its commitment to innovation. Yet the reality is usually different. Innovation labs, for example, may exist, yet further inspection often finds them to be isolated initiatives or divorced from the mainstream business.

The true test of how receptive an organization is in encouraging an experimental or intrapreneurial approach is hidden. It is the underlying, unstated culture of how the business actually operates that tells the real story, rather than PR-slanted declarations of 'fostering innovation and creativity'. It is reflected in the degree to which senior managers tolerate failure and risk-taking and how they champion innovative ideas. In simple terms, it is what organizations and the people within them *do* rather than what they *say*.

Our message to intrapreneurs and experimentalists is to ignore the rhetoric and start from the 'worst-case' scenario. They should begin by assuming that the business and its managers are highly risk-averse, and that failure is not an option. They should assume that time and resources are unlikely to be available and that senior-level sponsorship for an experiment or idea will not be forthcoming.

Taking this perspective means that the intrapreneur will not make the mistake of believing that their own passion for ideas is shared by everybody else. By assuming the 'worst case', they will go the extra mile to develop the relationships and make the compelling business case to overcome irrational resistance. The following checklist can help with developing that business case.

The intrapreneur's checklist

1. Be the rebel with a cause

By their nature, intrapreneurs and experimentalists will be curious. There is something of the heretic about them as they question settled habits and challenge accepted practices. This can create discomfort among others and that means being sensitive to the ethics of their actions. The business case will help to justify the logic of the actions, but the experimentalist needs to do more than provide a stark rationale. They also need to convince people of their altruism, and that their proposal is for the organizational benefit, if they are to avoid accusations of being 'self-promoters' or 'disruptors'. Failure to do so will mean the experiment or idea not even starting.

2. Get a senior-level sponsor

Having a senior-level sponsor from the early days will make the intrapreneur's or experimentalist's cause a lot easier. We place it high on the checklist since, without such sponsorship, the experiment or idea is unlikely to go anywhere. The sponsor needs to be someone who has a business interest in the outcomes but should not direct the process. They will be someone who can raise the visibility of the experiment or idea, work across functions' boundaries and procure resources where necessary. They can act as a coach and as a 'client' to ensure that the idea or experiment retains its focus on business value. Finally, they can be the promoter of next steps by giving more weight to the proposals and recommendations.

3. Be seen as a doer, not a dreamer

In many organizations, intrapreneurs and experimentalists can be dismissed as idealistic or unrealistic. In others, their ideas are seen as disruptive or, at best, distractions from the 'day job' and from the main purpose of the organization. In either setting it means it can be difficult to give an idea the visibility it requires. The senior-level sponsor can help to open doors, but that is only part of the process. Once through the door, the intrapreneur needs to have a compelling message. This is not just about quantifying the costs and benefits or demonstrating that the risks will be managed with care, it is more than that. The intrapreneur should be able to demonstrate the practical aspects of how they will test their idea – the *how*, *where* and *when* of the experiment or proposal. It is at this stage that the six-step process we describe in later chapters can help to shape a practical proposition.

4. Share the pain and grief

The business case will need to explain why the experiment or idea should be supported. It needs to provide the financial costs and other penalties of *not* going ahead. At the same time, it needs to lay out the hard facts about the potential for adding value to the business. When senior managers see the penalties and potential benefits laid out in quantitative terms, it makes their decisions much easier. A manager we worked with in a Spanish bank tried hard to get approval for an experiment to improve customer retention. His proposals led to nothing until he showed how the financial costs were impacting the two-year growth plan.

5. Identify risks and fears early

Too often we have observed intrapreneurs and experiment teams misled by early enthusiasm for an idea. The enthusiastic conversations that begin with 'that sounds a great idea – count me in' often evaporate when the risks or the practical demands become clearer to those involved. Part of 'selling' the idea will be to adopt the 'worst-case' perspective that we highlighted earlier. This means recognizing the greatest concerns of individuals and demonstrating how they will be managed. It is important at this stage to also recognize that the risks for one person may be different from another. Identifying risks early and showing how they will be mitigated will also provide more confidence among potential sponsors and likely participants.

6. Don't try to boil the ocean

The topic idea is almost certainly the most contentious issue for an experimentalist and is integral to people's perceptions of risk and the impact of failure. Our advice to the newcomer is not to try to change the world in one go. They may have a big idea that can have organizational impact, but they should look at ways of introducing it in a contained way. It is here that the experimentation process can help. When talking with Satoshi about choosing a topic that would help him to introduce the concept of experimentation in his organization, we suggested that he choose a topic that:

- deals with a recognized problem or opportunity;
- has an internal focus, where scope and risk can be managed more effectively. This may include:
  - people – such as new ways of working, recruitment, engagement;
  - performance – such as process and system improvements;
  - profitability – such as cost reductions, staff efficiencies;
- has a short duration – where results and impact can be measured in four to six months;
- has a limited call on the resources of time and people – and where the resources are within your own control;
- can be conducted in a contained area, such as a single function or location with limited cross-boundary involvement;
- can be replicated and therefore have significance across the wider organization.

7. Get people on board

One of the most important challenges for the intrapreneur or the individual experimentalist is building a cadre of fellow enthusiasts. The big mistake we observe in these situations is that inevitably the 'enthusiasts' are exactly that! In such situations, the idea or experiment topic can be swept along on a tide of excitement and positivity. It means that risks and obstacles may be diminished and overlooked as the prospect of a game-changing intervention beckons. It is unrealistic to recruit 'doubters' to the team, but the cadre needs to develop processes by which they can challenge themselves and play devil's advocate. The templates we provide in the experiment process are designed to do exactly that and to avoid groupthink.

For an experimentalist like Satoshi, there are two groups to consider. The first is the immediate experiment team, who are likely to be the cadre of enthusiasts. This small group of four or five people will have a vested interest in the outcome of the experiment. They may be members of the management team or direct reports or simply colleagues. The second group to influence is the one that will be taking part in the experiment. This population will either be involved as members of the experiment and control groups or be impacted in some way by the outcome. In both cases, there will be a responsibility on the individual experimentalist to educate the groups on the philosophy and approach to experimentation. Engaging the experiment groups at the earliest stage has been a proven way of creating ownership of the process.

Further support for the intrapreneur and individual experimentalist is provided in the following downloadable guides:

- Creating the business case:

DOWNLOAD at www.koganpage.com/BusExp

Guide – OR8. Topic selection criteria

- Identifying risks and degree of complexity:

DOWNLOAD at www.koganpage.com/BusExp

Guide – OR7. Managing risk and complexity

- Introduction to the concepts and practice of experimentation:

DOWNLOAD at www.koganpage.com/BusExp

Guide – OR0. Introduction to experimentation

- Getting people on board:

DOWNLOAD at www.koganpage.com/BusExp

Guide – OR3. Topic selection workshop

The small business entrepreneur

By definition, the small business entrepreneur is unencumbered by the hierarchies and bureaucracies that we have just described. If they are the owner or a senior manager, the task of introducing experimentation or innovative ideas is easier… but still not straightforward.

A small business entrepreneur has the additional advantages of being much closer to the customer or end user and being able to respond to their changing needs more quickly. An illustration of that agility is illustrated in the GetApp Business Model survey conducted in the USA in June 2020. It highlights how small businesses have adapted to consumer behaviour during the pandemic. It revealed that 92 per cent of those surveyed had fundamentally changed their business model in less than four months in at least one of the areas shown in Figure 5.1. These are not the short-term examples of innovation we described earlier where Mercedes/McLaren produced ventilators, but significant shifts in the way they have committed to do business in the future.

In most cases, the businesses surveyed were faced with existential threats. They were compelled to adapt because there were few alternatives. They had to take big risks or invest scarce resources to make the necessary changes that may not have been their first choice.

FIGURE 5.1 Business model pivots in response to Covid-19

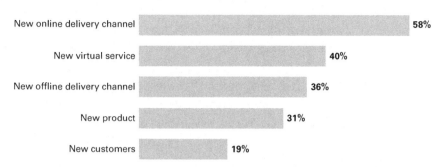

QUESTION: Which of the above describes a business model pivot your company has made in response to Covid-19? Select all that apply. N: 577.

SOURCE GetApp Business Model Survey[1]

In some ways, the whole experience might be seen as a compression of the 'normal' business rhythm. Customers' needs will frequently change, competitors can gain advantage, supply chains and delivery channels can be disrupted... but this happened almost overnight and with little warning.

The discussions we have had with small business owners is that risking the entire company is not an option they want to repeat. However, it has been a reminder of the need to stay one step ahead of competitors, to anticipate changes in customer needs, to protect routes to market and to explore the benefits of new products and services.

This is fertile territory for experimentation and why we see it as such a powerful tool for the small business entrepreneur. Instead of having to 'bet the farm', they can start to 'farm their bets'. Every small business will have its unique set of circumstances, but the following case study provides insights into how one business followed an experimental approach.

CASE STUDY
The small business owner

Beachdale is a family firm of kitchen furniture suppliers in the south of England. They employ about 50 people in their main warehouses and provide flat-pack kitchen units to both small and large retailers and builders' merchants across the region. In 2016, and with the business growing, they became increasingly aware of the risks to their planned development. Their reliance on a single supplier of cupboard and cabinet units not only restricted their growth but was also holding them hostage to price increases, product availability and changing routes to markets.

Stephen Andrews, the managing director, had already had his own thoughts about solutions but wanted to draw even more ideas from his management team. The initial get-together produced a wealth of ideas, some of which Stephen admitted were 'way off-the-wall', but the session had been fun as well as productive. The managers felt that, as they had benefited from the experience, they wanted to involve their own teams in similar discussions.

At the lunchtime 'sandwich sessions', the managers observed a very different side to their colleagues than they had seen before. Louise Brown, the operations manager, commented on the energy and how the ideas came tumbling out, with one building on the other. The employees' reactions to being involved were also surprising. One of the workshop team told their manager, 'I've always enjoyed working here but now it feels like a *real* family firm. It feels like we're doing this together.'

The management team gathered all the ideas and established a set of criteria to filter their final choices. The priority was selecting ideas that could reduce the supply chain risks. Opportunities to diversify into supplying kitchen appliances and offering a design service were seen as worth exploring but were never going to match the revenue of the core business. The idea the team selected as the most feasible was to continue to buy in the cabinets as flat-pack, find doors that could be own-branded and assemble the units in-house before distribution to the client. Sourcing the component parts from a variety of manufacturers meant the main issue of supply chain control would be addressed. However, it would also require a significant shift in the warehouse capacity and that, in turn, would require additional investment in new tooling as well as end-product marketing support.

Stephen and the management team knew that betting the farm on the idea would not only be costly but would have existential risks. Instead, they decided to run an experiment that would test their in-house capability, explore the costs, survey customer reaction and explore pricing thresholds. Their hypothesis was:

> By producing own-branded rigid kitchen furniture, we will reduce the reliance on individual suppliers, improve profitability and provide high-quality, affordable products for existing and new customers.

The team gave themselves three months to test the hypothesis. They set up a discrete part of the existing warehouse as a cabinet assembly area. They negotiated contracts with new door suppliers and surveyed their customer base to test reactions. As a small business, undertaking this type of experiment was never going to be easy. Resources were always going to be stretched. The demands of the 'day job' had still to be met and existing customers still needed to be satisfied. Similarly, a small business cannot divert resources from one area to another in the way a larger business can. There is simply not the capacity or, in this case, the depth of people with the skills required for cabinet assembly.

Stephen felt it important to keep everybody on board and, once the decision was made to go ahead with the own-brand assembly idea, he called the whole workforce together. He wanted to explain the management team's appreciation of their ideas and how they had all been part of the process. Clearly not everyone was involved, and he was surprised how, in the following weeks, he was constantly being stopped around the warehouse and asked about progress. He decided to maintain the momentum and keep the interest going by asking the managers to provide short updates of the experiment during their weekly meetings.

After three months, the team evaluated the results. The hypothesis was only partly proven.

They had proven that they could produce in-house, own-branded cabinets and cupboards at a quality equal to (and even better than) their existing supplier. However, despite their initial costings and market-testing, the experiment revealed that the actual costs of production were higher than expected. An economy of scale would be required to meet a price that small retailers would pay, and they were never going to buy in sufficient quantities. The team was disappointed but, despite a largely disproven hypothesis, they felt the experiment approach had succeeded in many ways:

- It had avoided excessive investment.
- It had provided confidence that Beachdale did have the skills and capabilities to produce the products.
- It demonstrated that they *could* take that route if the order quantity and consistency justified the additional investment in space and machinery.
- New ideas had emerged around diverse product offerings that were being implemented.
- And finally, the family business now felt like a 'family' at all levels.

A month after the end of the experiment, the sales manager telephoned Stephen excitedly. He had just spoken with a developer who required kitchen units for

180 houses they were building on the south coast. They both realized that this was the opportunity that they had been waiting for that would allow them to produce the units profitably. The contract was signed and a new business model for Beachdale was set in motion.

Stephen commented afterwards, 'We may have ended up with a disproven hypothesis, but if it had not been for our experiment, we would never have been in a position, nor would we have had the confidence, to have grasped the opportunity.'

This type of experiment is a good example of a prototype or mock-up and depends less on the 'scientific' aspects that we describe in other types, such as A/B testing. While that might mean less attention being paid to extraneous variables and like-for-like comparisons, the experiment still needs to provide robust data on which business decisions can be made with a degree of confidence. This experiment achieved that and did more to exemplify an experimental approach in tune with the six-step model:

- IDENTIFY. It began with a well-identified problem.

- DISCOVER. Stephen and his team spent time examining the problem in greater depth to confirm the level of risk and its potential impact on business growth and security.

- IDEATE. The experiment engaged a broad cross-section of employees in the development of ideas and solutions. It also explored beyond the business to gain views of customers and potential suppliers.

- DEFINE. The team filtered the ideas using a distinct set of criteria to assess the shortlisted ideas and then formulated a clearly defined hypothesis.

- EXPERIMENT. They set up an experiment 'site' to test their hypothesis and monitored progress over an agreed timescale. They were careful to communicate progress to the wider community not immediately involved.

- EVALUATE. The results allowed them to make a business decision that, without the experiment, may have incurred significant financial and resource costs.

Summary

This chapter has focused on the individual experimentalist. We have viewed the experimentalist through two lenses. First, we have highlighted the challenges often faced by the intrapreneur and provided examples of well-known innovations that had experienced lengthy struggles through organizational bureaucracy and inertia. We then provided tactics in the form of a checklist that the intrapreneur can use to overcome some of the organizational obstacles in getting their ideas heard. The second part of the chapter focused on the entrepreneur or small business owner. In this setting the experimentalist can be much nimbler and more agile. They will almost certainly have greater influence within the business and are invariably closer to the customer. We closed the chapter with a case study to illustrate how the six-step methodology can be applied just as successfully in a small business as in a large company.

In the next chapter we look at opportunities for experimentation that best lend themselves to experimentation.

Note

1 Capers, Z (23 July 2020) America's small businesses have reinvented themselves – and it's paying off, GetApp, https://www.getapp.com/resources/business-model-change/ (archived at https://perma.cc/FU6Z-LE98)

06

The experimentalist:
Attitudes and assumptions

It was late afternoon in London but past midnight in Beijing as we listened to Stefan, the country manager in a medical diagnostics business, talk about his group's experiment progress with increasing frustration. He was an experienced clinician and an accomplished business leader with a track record of success, and yet he was explaining how he had never felt so out of control. His irritation was focused on the experiment process and how it was demanding a very different set of behaviours from those he had been used to. As a medical man, accustomed to the clinical purity of experiments, he was also finding it difficult to apply our notion of a scientific approach to experimentation in a business setting. He asked: 'I'm used to clinical trials, so how scientific do we really need to be?'

That call of 10 years ago sticks in our minds. Similar conversations over the years have made us re-evaluate how we prepare managers for experimentation. Of course, it has been important to explain the process and inspire people with other examples of business experiments, but we were failing to manage their expectations of the change in mindset that was required. We were explaining what people needed to *do* but not explaining how they would *feel*. It became apparent to us that the behavioural, emotional and intellectual challenges of experimentation were as important to a successful outcome as a rigorous application of the process. Similarly, we observed the frequency of the question, 'How scientific is scientific?' to which we will return later in the book. In this chapter, we shall focus on behaviours and mindset.

Dispelling the managerial myths

Our client organizations often see experimentation as a way of promoting innovation and agility in their business and yet, too often, we see them rewarding managerial practices that encourage the opposite. Experimentation requires an adjustment in most managers' beliefs and behaviours. It is a shift away from some of the accepted, more traditional managerial practices and beliefs. We saw from Stefan and others that this is not an easy transition to make. The existing practices are often so entrenched that they become an invisible part of the fabric of the organization – almost mythical in their status.

That does not mean totally dismissing the beliefs or discarding the practices – they will be appropriate in other situations. It is more about dispelling them *in an experimental context*. In doing so we can manage expectations better and help individuals prepare for those changes.

Here we have picked out some of the key changes. Expressed as 'myths', they encapsulate a number of traditional attitudes and practices that *may* still persist, but which can be either irrelevant or even counterproductive in an experimental setting.

Myth: Failure is a sin

The whole point of experimentation is that failure will happen – so accept it. From our earliest school days, we are conditioned to pass or fail examinations. In work we are expected to present a track record of success if we are to be rewarded and recognized with promotion. There is rarely space for 'failure', and yet that is central to the spirit of experimentation. The list of quotes by entrepreneurs and inventors about the importance of accepting failure is lengthy, but Henry Ford's comment over one hundred years ago sums up the experimental mindset: 'The only real mistake is the one from which we learn nothing.' In experimentation, success is not about simply proving a hypothesis and 'failure' is not about a disproven hypothesis. It is what we do with the information gained that determines the difference. A disproven hypothesis can sometimes save a business a fortune by avoiding a costly mistake or it can lead to better solutions as other options are explored.

If we *are* to talk about 'failure' in an experiment setting, it should be focused on the process of gaining the information. Where an experiment has not generated robust data, or where it needed more rigour, or where the analysis was unsound, it can be justifiably considered to be 'failing'. However, real failure is not recognizing and learning from such deficiencies.

Myth: Leadership has the answers

Few organizations are truly democratic. Most of the large organizational structures, and even smaller ones, are legacies of the management theories from the early 20th century. Despite that, very few leaders or businesses would describe themselves as being autocratic or overly hierarchical in the way they operate. 'My door is always open.' 'We are always seeking people's feedback and opinions.' 'Our town-hall meetings are always lively and well attended.' These are just some of the things we hear as managers illustrate democratic principles in action. Their intentions are good, but what is *not* noticed is the assumption that *permission* is being given for the free expression of ideas. These are controlled and passive situations rather than a way of doing business informally and openly on a daily basis. While providing a veneer of democracy, it serves to reinforce a culture of hierarchy at odds with the principles of experimentation. In an experiment context, humility and a democratic impulse are central attributes of a leader or management team. They promote an environment in which people are comfortable being challenged and encourage others to do the same.

In terms of adjustments in behaviour, the challenge for leaders is to recognize their fallibility without losing face. As a starting point, it may mean the team leader ring-fencing the experiment process to create an environment in which status is suspended. By doing so, it creates a climate of open dialogue and mutual challenge before reverting to normal, non-experimental behaviour. Gradually the distinction is eroded and experimentation becomes an accepted way of working. We have encouraged leaders to do this as part of an 'experiment within an experiment'. They found that the quality of suggestions, solutions and ideas from those they had previously underestimated came as a surprise. Moving between the experimental and 'normal' settings gradually became seamless. They also found that using this approach created high levels of ownership by engaging those involved as equals from the beginning.

Myth: Risk needs to be minimized

The UK Atomic Energy Authority is one of the most regulated organizations in the world. When discussing risk with their managers, we were quickly able to fill several flipcharts of potential danger. When we started to analyse them, looking for realistic ways to mitigate or eliminate risk, we emerged with just two cases of genuine concern. In simple terms, one was to avoid any risk to health and the other was to avoid risks that might financially impact the company. This was a simplistic exercise but highlights the point we want to make. There are many rules, systems and processes that are rarely questioned as they are seen to protect against risk. Yet we are often mistaken. Sometimes we can be influenced by 'legacy' risks that are no longer relevant yet have a subconscious impact on our decision-making. In an experimental setting we look to explore those risks in a responsible way. Experimentation is about taking risk safely. As we shall see later, the degree of freedom within this framework can be adjusted to suit the situation and the level of perceived risk. It is an adjustable boundary that can encourage experimentation.

Myth: Management is the art of control

In our conversation with Stefan, it was the feeling that he had little control over events that created such anxiety. It is rare that any individual or team feels comfortable when faced with a lack of clarity and, at the start of an experiment, it can be particularly frustrating when answers are not immediately available. We see teams seeking comfort by drawing upon familiar practices, such as a clearly sign-posted project plan, to create a sense of order and control. However, the inescapable fact about experimentation is that a level of ambiguity and uncertainty will be a regular presence and control is often difficult. This is particularly true at the beginning of the process, but there will continue to be unanswered questions throughout the experiment.

It is also true that too much control at these stages can stifle innovation and inhibit an experimental mindset. The more that individuals and experiment teams strive to exert control in these early phases, the less time is spent on inquiry and generating creative options. We sometimes challenge teams by paraphrasing the quote from Mario Andretti, the racing driver: 'If everything seems under control, then you're just not going far enough.' Our role is to encourage individuals and teams to stay longer with ambiguity and uncertainty. In the early stages, we urge them to use divergent styles of thinking, opening up possibilities and brainstorming ideas, and not to converge too quickly upon a pragmatic 'project' approach.

Myth: Quicker decisions get better results

One of the biggest challenges we encounter, particularly with executive-level experiment teams, is their drive to get quick solutions to a problem. Organizations and individuals are used to seeking answers rather than asking questions: getting things done and moving on quickly to the next challenge. It is how most managers will have earned recognition and attained their current position, thereby reinforcing these behaviours. By contrast, experimentation means slowing down the process. This is counterintuitive and frustrating for many managers.

When working recently with a group of senior oil and gas executives, we asked them to generate as many ideas as they could to resolve their chosen problem. They very quickly came up with 15 very good ideas that had potential to add significant value to the business. Unprompted, the group then went quickly into a self-imposed task mode. They felt compelled to select just one or two of these ideas. It was clear that they could not implement all the options, but whereas *we* had asked them to come up with ideas, *they* had resolved to move urgently to an early shortlist. The result was a quick prioritization exercise where the loudest voices carried the greatest influence and some excellent ideas were barely discussed. We encouraged them to take more time, to revisit their ideas the following day in a more considered way, while keeping their hastily made choices on the table. The following week we learned that they had selected two of the ideas that had been discarded earlier and chose three of the ideas for development by others in the business. Experiments can be short and sharp if quick feedback is required, but it is not always about 'quick fixes'. It will generally mean thinking more slowly.

PIT STOP CHALLENGE

We were running a leadership programme for senior executives and, as part of a 'fun day with a purpose', there was an activity to see how quickly two groups could change the wheels of a Formula 1 racing car. In the 10-minute planning session, each team of 8 began loudly with plenty of ideas thrown together and many other ideas ignored. The loudest voices shaped the plans and a decision was quickly taken about who should do what. They were in view of each other and had been informed that the average time for an F1 pit stop time was 2.4 seconds and the record was 1.8 seconds. It was quickly assumed to be a competitive environment. The first run saw each team produce times of around 30–40 seconds. The next planning stage was calmer and more thoughtful. The contributions that had been ignored previously became part of the discussion and lessons were drawn from the first round. The second run came to 20–25 seconds. The final times were 13 seconds and 15 seconds. The teams didn't need us to link the activity as a metaphor for the pattern of decision-making in their normal work environment. The first-round planning phase was obscured by 'noise'. Solutions and options were offered but many were ignored or not heard. Decisions were made quickly. The loudest voices won out. Groupthink dominated. 'That's exactly how our meetings go!!' one team member observed.

It would be a stretch to suggest that this was experimentation or 'try and test' in action, but as the teams reflected further they were able to draw some parallels. If the activity had stopped after the first run, the results would have been poor; but the teams learned that by trying out some ideas and learning from them, spending just 10 minutes extra to formulate a plan, assigning roles and exploring further options, they were able to improve their performance by 300 per cent. Our claim that 'thinking slow not fast' generally produces better results required no further reinforcement.

Myth: The status quo is sacrosanct

The rhetoric of many organizations includes exhortations to challenge orthodoxy and question existing strategy. In reality, however, management team meetings are too often dominated by routine agendas and safe dialogue. We observe a couple of reasons for the lack of robust debate. First, challenging the firm's orthodoxies might be seen as disloyal or disrespectful, particularly to the 'owner' of the process or strategy. Second, individuals are reluctant to be seen as 'troublemakers' and almost always have their personal challenges to prioritize. That is not to suggest we observe only acquiescent managers or that team meetings are always placid affairs. It is clearly not the case. But what we do see are organizations where challenge is encouraged in a passive manner – 'do chip in with any concerns and questions' – rather than pursued proactively as part of an embedded culture.

Experimentalists will often have a heretical streak. They are individuals who purposefully rock the boat and disrupt settled habits and accepted practices. It is therefore a more assertive and courageous approach that we advocate for managers adopting experimentation. Courage means being bold enough to question the status quo and to try something new, not relying solely on the old ways of doing things. As we work with individuals and experiment teams, we encourage individuals to become *positive disruptors*. If courage means being unafraid to challenge hierarchies and to query long-established processes or systems, it also means creating discomfort. The dilemma for the individual is how to be candid and honest without alienating key players in the process. It is a difficult influencing skill to develop but an important one in experimentation.

Myth: Perfectionism is a virtue

People will almost always want to do their best at work. They are used to striving for perfection and have been conditioned in the workplace to deliver to their ultimate ability. We would not discourage that, but we do see how it can stifle opportunities to experiment. It can also add an unwanted tier of complexity.

- **Stopping before starting.** When people see that testing something would require prohibitive time and resources to do it perfectly, they are unlikely even to embark on it. In our example of the oil and gas executives, the team discarded one idea because it looked 'all too difficult'. It was indeed a big idea, but it had the potential to add significant value to the business. We asked them, 'So what *can* you test?' This challenge caused them to scale down the big idea rather than abandoning it. In such cases it is often better to get part of the story and build the experiment narrative than to discard the whole book without even opening it. In such cases, as long as the experiment is conducted with the appropriate rigour, the data can provide a stepping stone to solving the bigger problem.

- **Not stopping.** On occasions we have seen the opposite to be true with teams striving for the perfect answer, not knowing when to stop or wanting to be 'absolutely sure'. Our challenge in such circumstances is to ask whether the additional time, costs and resources of this perfectionism can be justified. If the decision can be made with a 'reasonable degree of confidence', we suggest there is no need to indulge in any further 'experiment creep'.

Individuals and teams need to become accustomed to going ahead with something that may not provide a complete answer but which is 'just good enough' for the situation in hand.

Myth: Experiments are only for scientists

Throughout this book, we regularly return to the theme raised in Stefan's question about 'how scientific do we need to be?' Stefan was from a medical background and his perception of an experiment was imbued with the purity of laboratory testing. However, we have often heard the same view being expressed by non-clinicians. Some simple questions hardly require a randomized control trial. Other, more complex problems will need valid and reliable data if the ensuing managerial decisions are to be made with a reasonable degree of confidence. However, we have rarely encountered a business experiment that matches the rigour of a clinical trial. The word 'experiment' can therefore be a myth in its own right if not properly understood in its context, even inhibiting individuals and teams from embarking on any trial-and-error initiative.

Summary

In this chapter, we have highlighted a number of common practices and attitudes that can be irrelevant or even counterproductive in an experimental setting. We described them as 'myths' because they are so often embedded in the organizational fabric that they become invisible. Some may resonate more than others, and some may seem provocative, but the purpose has been to underline the behavioural adjustments required in experimentation. They are summarized in the box below.

DISPELLING THE MYTHS – 12 DOS AND DON'TS

1   DO accept that failure is an option. A disproven hypothesis is a success.

2   DO empower others. You will need them. Democratize the process.

3   DO advocate and demonstrate curiosity and questioning.

4   DO explore new ideas. Embrace different perspectives with a passion.

5 DO seek to challenge, and encourage others to challenge you.

6 DO take responsible risks – use experimentation as a licence to be bold.

7 DO NOT think *you* have to have all the answers – it is okay to be 'vulnerable'.

8 DO NOT fear ambiguity and uncertainty. They are part of the process.

9 DO NOT strive for control. It is an experiment, *not* a project.

10 DO NOT rush to decisions; enlarge the number of options.

11 DO NOT seek perfection – 80 per cent *may* be good enough.

12 DO NOT think experimentation is a scientific activity – it is a business activity.

By placing a spotlight on the behavioural adjustments early in the experiment process, there are a number of benefits:

- It manages expectations by providing advance warning of the potential challenges ahead. It means that people like Stefan are prepared and can respond.
- It promotes a 'policing' of the process by the teams themselves. They may begin to question whether they are taking enough risks or if they have lapsed too early into a 'project mindset'.
- It provides 'permission' for a robust discussion around the emotional highs and lows of the experimentation journey, resulting in much tighter team dynamics.

The last two chapters have discussed how you can influence experimentation in your own organization, either as a team member or a sole pioneer, making adjustments in your own behaviour accordingly.

In the next chapter, we address the wider opportunities for experimentation and share ideas that intrapreneurs and entrepreneurs typically have.

07

Exploring opportunities and creating choices

We described earlier how curiosity is a central tenet of experimentation. And yet, such enquiry inevitably raises more questions than answers. That is what teams encounter in the early IDENTIFY, DISCOVERY and IDEATE stages of the process. They uncover opportunities and topic choices that, being unexpected, add to an already ambiguous and uncertain situation.

It means that there are stages in the experiment process where teams are reluctant to extend their horizons further. They want to close down options and deal with what they already have, in order to feel more in control. Our major concern when working with managers is narrowness of thinking. The tools and techniques we describe in the six-step process are important in helping teams to create and filter their ideas. However, if those ideas are constrained by focusing too narrowly on their own experience, their own business and their own industry, they will fall short of the potential that experimentation can provide.

Experimentation is not simply about following a process but also about inspiring people. It can open eyes to new opportunities and possibilities. Our challenge as experiment tutors is to encourage people to go even further – to live longer with the ambiguity and uncertainty. We want them to gain the full benefits of the opportunities that experimentation can deliver and help them to make the best topic choices for *their* business.

This chapter describes four ways of achieving those two goals:

1 Draw **transferable lessons** from experiments across diverse businesses and sectors.

2 Apply a **typology of experiments** that provides easy comparison between common themes when choosing good topics.

3 Clarify choices around **risk and complexity**.

4 Illustrate how a **single methodology** can be applied to any topic choice.

This comparative approach plays an important part in the process. It opens managerial eyes to the breadth of opportunities for experiment topics. It provides an opportunity to learn from others. It inspires and emboldens people to be curious, and to question their own attitudes to risk and 'failure'.

In this chapter we focus on ways of extending horizons. Our aim is to encourage people to explore the OPPORTUNITIES beyond the familiar and gain more from an experimental approach to business decision-making.

1. Transferable lessons

We never fail to be surprised by how lessons can be drawn from even the most diverse industries and competitive environments. When working with experiment teams in one firm, we are keen to share the lessons learned and the choices made in other organizations. Here, we expand on two such insights and describe the ways they contribute to business experimentation.

A licence to experiment

Inspiring managers to experiment is not simply about describing ideas and topics that may be relevant, but also giving examples of courage. It is here that clients appreciate how others have pushed boundaries, how they have challenged entrenched ways of working and sought new opportunities. Using such comparisons they award themselves a tacit 'licence' to start thinking differently – to be more curious and inquisitive. The final topic choice will always rest with the experiment team, but we know when an experimental mindset is taking shape when we see managers enthusiastically sharing ideas and comments like: 'I wonder what would happen if...?', 'Why don't we try...?' 'We really need a new way of...' 'Maybe we could look at...' 'Wouldn't it be interesting to...?'. It becomes a platform from which teams can then move on to identify topics that have relevance in *their* business. These may include:

- exploring new ways of working;
- questioning and challenging organizational norms;
- viewing problems through fresh eyes;
- seeking improvements to processes and systems;
- identifying new services and products.

Learning from others

DISCOVERY is one of the stages of the six-step experimentation process. It is where learning from others is fundamental. In our work with clients, ranging from the chemical industry to financial services, we see many common challenges, such as improving sales processes, better recruitment and retention, and increased customer satisfaction.

Most clients accept the commonality of these issues and their relevance to their own business. However, we still observe a reluctance to widen horizons and learn from others when the problem or opportunity is less obviously linked. A comment from a client in the oil and gas industry reflects a generally held view:

> I'm struggling with improving our safety systems and I really can't see how I can learn lessons from a consultancy company improving sales processes.

All too often, in such situations, we see experiment teams confining their research and problem-solving to their own part of the business. It is rare to find them involving other units, functions or locations – even though these may be experiencing similar problems. When looking for potential solutions, going outside the company is rarer still. Too few consider what learning can be gained from other companies, competitors, as well as universities and professional bodies. And yet, this has proven to be such a rich source of new ideas, as the case study in Appendix D illustrates.

2. A typology of experiments

Early in our work, we recognized that the reticence to extend horizons was influencing the quality of experiments. Topic choices and potential solutions were simply too narrow. People were choosing to stick with tried and tested methods. For all the interest in what others were doing, it rarely translated to active exploration or deeper research. We decided that if we wanted to promote the DISCOVERY phase of experimentation using a comparative approach, we had to do something differently. We had to make the commonality more obvious and the opportunities to learn even more accessible. In short, we had to make it an easy CHOICE to extend horizons.

It is for that reason we developed a 'typology' of experiments, most of which can almost always be categorized into three 'types' defined by their PURPOSE:

- problem-solving;
- performance improvement;
- disruptive (or strategic) innovation.

We expand on the three themes and the typology in the next section, as they provide an accessible framework to compare opportunities for topic choices and to learn from others. In terms of raising awareness, it also provides a useful reference point for people like our earlier oil and gas client. A safety topic and a sales topic are clearly different, but they also share many characteristics and can benefit from the same experimental approach to improving processes.

Expanding the three themes

In this section, we provide case examples for each of the three categories. How are these categories different?

Experiments in the 'problem-solving' category are usually those addressing current issues that, if not fixed, could have a detrimental impact on the business. By comparison, an experiment in the 'performance' category concerns something that is working satisfactorily but where its potential is underexploited.

The third category, 'strategic' innovation, is where the experiment is exploring an opportunity that differs significantly from existing business models, markets, products and services. In this case its impact is likely to be longer term, less operational and external to the business. We also use the term 'disruptive' to capture the idea that these experiments may have an impact on wider industry or society in general. Table 7.1 summarizes the three types of experiment. The right-hand column reinforces the message that all three types can be handled by a single process.

A. PROBLEM-SOLVING EXPERIMENTS

There is usually an immediacy about these types of experiments. They are particularly suited to situations that require short-term operational solutions. The first is where a problem has just arisen that has rarely been encountered before. The second is where a persistent problem is beginning to have a deleterious impact on growth and ambition. In both cases, tried and tested solutions and traditional responses have not provided the answers. Something new is required. Here are two examples.

TABLE 7.1 A typology of business experiments

Purpose of experimentation	Type of innovation	Business benefits	Identical process
Problem-solving Addressing new or recurring problems	**Operational innovation** Experiments generally focus on new or recurring problems within the organization and mainly have localized impact.	**Marginal gains** Can produce incremental benefits that, if accumulated, lead to major progress or lasting solutions. Although experiments may be focused internally, they often result in benefits to external stakeholders.	Explore and research the problem or opportunity
Performance improvement Processes and people	**Operational innovation** Experiments generally split into improving performance of internal processes and systems or the performance and engagement of people.	**Marginal gains** As above – can produce incremental benefits leading to significant changes. Although experiments may be focused internally, there are often benefits to clients and other stakeholders.	Seek a range of options and ideas to solve or exploit it
Testing new or different: • business models; • value propositions; • clients & stakeholders; • products and services; • delivery processes.	**Disruptive (strategic) innovation** These experiments are aimed at exploring opportunities that can result in significant departures from current value propositions, customers or delivery channels.	**Major gains** Benefits here can result in step changes in service offerings, new markets and clients to gain competitive advantage. They have the potential to impact strategic decision-making.	Formulate a hypothesis, test it and learn from it Succeed or learn from the failure

EXAMPLE 1

A new problem

A Swiss-based medical diagnostic firm was faced with a blood-sampling machine that was becoming unreliable. Replacement parts were held in storage in Germany and were taking up to 18 days to arrive from the warehouse via traditional methods to the medical centre in a remote part of Brazil. This meant thousands of important blood tests were being delayed. While this was an immediate problem to be addressed, it also caused the team to challenge the wider picture – the costs of inventory management and logistics. The team took the view that solving the immediate problem was critical for patients' health but that a longer-term solution was also required. They conducted an experiment to test their hypothesis that using a 3D printing method for fragile instrument parts would create savings in delivery time and costs. Despite significant regulatory, legal and technical obstacles, the team successfully produced the replacement part in Brazil by 3D printing. They reduced the 18 days' delivery time to just 3 hours with minimal costs. In addition, they found that 12,000 (or two-thirds) of the inventory items in Germany were 'slow-moving' parts (ordered twice a year or less) and could benefit from 3D printing. The team estimated that 1,500 items were sufficiently high cost for 3D printing to be financially competitive and projected potential net savings of 21 per cent (or $12 million a year) on inventory control and delivery.

EXAMPLE 2

A recurring problem

Challenged by the low unemployment rate and tough competition for talent on the West Coast of the USA, an HR organization faced a persistent problem with engagement and retention. The tried and tested 'tweaks' were making little headway and the problem was starting to impact their two-year growth plan. They assessed that the costs of disruption to client relationships, the loss of knowledge caused by those leaving and the costs of onboarding new staff were becoming business-critical. The management team decided they had to try something different through experimentation. An important part of this experiment was the way in which the team researched the problem itself. They discovered that 70 per cent of the staff turnover was preventable and that the main retention problem was among their biggest revenue earners, who were contributing up to $1 million gross profit per person. They also reached out for new ideas as previous ones were making little difference. They engaged with their own people and learned what they could from other parts of their organization. They also researched leading practice in other organizations. They identified a number of companies on the West Coast, to see how they were handling similar regional challenges (including Starbucks, Apple, Amazon, Google, Expedia and Microsoft). They also contacted universities and professional bodies to gain a better understanding of what they *could* try. The result was an impressive portfolio of 35 ideas to test experimentally. They prioritized them and expressed them as testable hypotheses. From the ensuing experiment results, they were able to reduce turnover of staff in San Francisco from 76 per cent to 26 per cent and in Seattle from 40 per cent to 30 per cent in a single year.

In *both* examples it is worth noting that an individual problem unearthed a larger systemic issue in the experimentation process, that, in turn, resulted in a wider process improvement across the organization.

B. PERFORMANCE IMPROVEMENT EXPERIMENTS

Like problem-solving, this can easily be broken down into two areas. The first is about processes – getting the best from existing systems or looking at better ways of introducing new technology. The second is around people performance, and that can range from experimenting with new ways of rewarding people to improving well-being in the workplace.

EXAMPLE 3

Process improvement

Introducing new technology in any organization is demanding of both managers and employees, and in our experience can almost always be done better. It was this that sparked the imagination of a Dutch-based consultancy firm who were introducing an app to enable data-driven sales and improve commercial performance. Adoption of new processes in the organization had not been successful in the past, with top–down communication extolling the benefits and encouraging (or requiring) people to use the new systems. The team wanted to try out something different. They set up an experiment with a control group that experienced the traditional rollout process, and the experiment group, where the team engaged the end-users in 'quick sprints' through weekly scrums where they had a say in what needed to be in the app and how it could be used. The team recognized very quickly that this was not as much an experiment about new technology but one that was about 'behavioural change', and they were mindful how the process was countercultural in a number of ways. First, the organization was used to getting things 100 per cent correct and then rolling something out, so this process of gradual improvement and running with something part-completed was a challenge. Second, involving employees at a very early stage to gain their contributions and ownership was opposite to the previous top–down approach. The results of the experiment over a five-month period were so successful in Holland that the same process was used when rolling out the new technology to other parts of the business – in Europe initially and then globally.

People performance

This is one of the most popular kinds of business experiments since it can be conducted simply and quickly. They can be much lower risk and often less complex than other experiments and are a good starting point for those new to experimentation. To illustrate the principal areas of focus, we have grouped 'people' experiments under a number of headings:

- organizational culture;
- relationships, processes and dynamics;
- performance management (people);
- recruitment, engagement and retention.

Appendix C provides an expanded version of topics under each of these headings with over 30 cases of 'people' experiments. Two are selected here.

EXAMPLE 4

Performance management (people)

Not every experiment will corroborate the hypothesis. Here is an example where the hypothesis was 'not proven' and yet where the experiment itself made a significant contribution to a wider organizational debate about performance management. The genesis of the experiment was based on anecdotal evidence and intuition that performance ratings and statistical distributions were an ineffective element of the performance management system. In particular, they were suspected of being demotivating. The team started with a bold approach – they wanted to remove the existing process and replace it with regular one-to-one manager meetings dedicated to performance and development. Phase one began with surveys and interviews to provide a better qualitative understanding of the anecdotal evidence. The team also researched a number of other organizations, such as Deloitte, Microsoft and Expedia, that were also grappling with the same question: 'Does our current performance management approach achieve employee motivation and engagement?' At the outset, they had gained tacit approval from both the HR and legal functions and had identified locations where they could run the experiment. The team experienced many twists and turns on the journey. They showed resilience and determination and learned a lot about influencing across organizational boundaries. But, with final approval not forthcoming and experiment timings beginning to overlap with the 'normal' annual performance cycle, the team was unable to fully test their hypothesis. However, phase one had confirmed an important problem in the business that had previously been 'under the radar' and deserved greater attention. The experiment produced valuable statistical evidence that tested the question above and within 12 months the organization revisited the issue using that evidence.

EXAMPLE 5

Relationships, processes and dynamics

The team set out to prove that transparency of decision-making has an impact on the quality of decisions and employee engagement. They researched the topic widely with a key statistic in their minds that organizations with higher engagement are 78 per cent more productive and 40 per cent more profitable. They decided to test it out in their medium-sized manufacturing company and set up a control group and two experiment groups that were comparable in terms of numbers and decision-making responsibilities. They were careful to ensure they had base measures on the three main areas of focus: employee engagement, decision-making performance and employee understanding of the corporate strategy. They ran the experiment for three months. The experiment groups used additional techniques to communicate and provide greater transparency. The control group used the normal practices of communicating decisions. The result was that the number of decisions in the experiment group increased in comparison with the control group and were 30 per cent better in quality. The employee engagement scores increased by 20 per cent. The team was satisfied that the experiment corroborated the hypothesis. However, the team was aware that the experiment was also about gaining better insights into the type of content and the medium of communication that was needed to improve upon the 'dumping' of information on people. The results have now been applied across the business with a similar impact on engagement scores.

C. STRATEGIC (DISRUPTIVE) EXPERIMENTS

The first two categories of experiment, dealing with problems and performance, are largely focused on operational innovation where short-term solutions are expected. While the outcomes may in the end benefit or influence customers or external stakeholders, the experiments themselves are more internally focused with changes impacting the organization. When we categorize experiments as 'strategic' or 'disruptive', it is because their impact will, in most cases, be external to the organization and usually measured in the longer term.

Typically experiments in this category are looking at new or significantly different:

- client or stakeholder groups;
- market segments;
- products or services;

- business models or value propositions;
- delivery channels.

A further distinction with these types of experiments is that they have the capacity to create major breakthroughs in innovation that, in turn, raise important questions about the direction of the business. By contrast, the business benefits created by the other two categories are usually incremental, producing only marginal gains.

We use two examples here from Roche, the pharmaceutical company, to illustrate strategic experiments, sometimes with unexpected benefits. Appendices D and E provide more detailed versions of each case study.

EXAMPLE 6
Different stakeholders and new products/services

Game Changing Innovation was prompted by an experiment group that wanted to explore 'the next big thing' by seeking new perspectives from a population very different from those inside the organization. They formulated their question as follows: 'Are we missing out on the disruptive or unconventional ideas – the true game changers – that could help us reach our purpose?' They hit upon a novel way of answering it. 'We had the bright idea of asking the next generation – the current graduate students – people untainted by our company and its biases, with (hopefully) a fresh point of view.' They wanted to find young scientists who were not influenced by a corporate mindset – people who had an open mind on potential game changers in the next 10–20 years. Their hypothesis was that by sourcing ideas from aspiring young scientists, they would identify promising opportunities for Roche. It was not just about generating ideas, but testing new ways of innovating outside of the established Roche processes. Gaining access to the younger population was difficult at first. Things turned around when they partnered with a UK-based corporate university networking organization that had access to thousands of students worldwide. The team offered a £5,000 prize for the best idea and the competition was opened to 93 universities in 28 countries. Although nearly half of the responses were unrelated to Roche's areas of interest, there were still 138 ideas that met the criteria. Those who were shortlisted were invited to present their ideas in Basel. The winner was a highly unusual idea for 3D bio-printed smart red blood cells, but the experiment also yielded several other benefits.

It enhanced the reputation of Roche in the eyes of universities, who admired the initiative, and it was also a massive talent scouting opportunity. The top 18 participants in the competition were approached by Roche in their respective countries and several job offers ensued. The innovation department continued to liaise with the participants and there are plans to repeat the experiment in coming years.

EXAMPLE 7

New value proposition

Pay what you want was sparked by a combination of the group's interest in a 'freemium' sales model and the launch of a new blood diagnostic test in Germany that assessed two cardiovascular risks (lipid levels and glucose levels). As blood tests were traditionally carried out by GPs in Germany, there were initial barriers to the idea, so they chose to focus upon pharmacies. They decided to try out an innovative pricing concept for patients: 'pay whatever you want.' Pharmacies were provided with the equipment free on loan and were invited to make the following offer to patients: 'we will deliver this service, after which you can decide what you are willing to pay.' The hypothesis was that such an approach might bring in less revenue per test, but the higher volume of tests would more than compensate, along with the obvious benefits to public health. The team identified 'anchor' prices that could be revealed by pharmacies as a guide, if the patients asked for one. The experiment lasted for three months. The results found that offering single-risk (lipid OR glucose) tests was more profitable than offering both tests and that it reduced the time for results by 50 per cent. They also learned about how the anchor price range impacts the contribution. A further experiment was conducted in Italy at GP surgeries using a control group and with the experiment group averaging €4 less per test. In both Germany and Italy, the team expected a reduction in revenue per test, as many people paid nothing, but the experiment demonstrated that different price positioning and framing by testing staff was able to balance that. The other part of the hypothesis was opening access to healthcare to a wider audience and over 300 people took part. The team found that 24 people (1 in 12) were discovered to be in a high-risk category who, without the offer of a 'pay what you want test', would be unaware of their condition. The team then began working with executives in the diagnostics business unit to build on their learning to see how a version of the experiment could be trialled more widely.

3. Risk and complexity

We explained earlier that, in addition to inspiring people with the breadth of ideas and topics, the comparative approach raises their curiosity. As they hear about the boldness of other experiments, they begin to question their own attitudes to risk. The experiment examples in the previous section were sparked by managers challenging the standard way of doing things and taking risks in doing so. Whether the experiment process was driven by an urgent problem or trying out a new business model, it meant that teams had to consider the risks relating to the complexity of their topic options. They had to make their choices by considering the risks of the logistical and resource challenges. They had to answer the question: 'Can we actually do this?' Beyond the risks associated with the practical management of the experiment, there are also concerns relating to the level of business and reputational risk. This may seem obvious when considering externally facing experiments, but is often overlooked with internal experiments.

As with topic choice, there will need to be choices made about the degree of challenge and risk they are prepared to accept. In earlier chapters, newcomers were advised to select low-risk, low-complexity topics as a way of becoming familiar with the six-step process before moving on to more complex situations. However, experimentation is intrinsically risky and experienced groups are encouraged to be more courageous and to push the boundaries of risk and complexity. But what do we mean by the boundaries, what are the risks and what is meant by a complex situation in an experiment?

The downloadable guide provides a template for helping teams to assess their topic(s) alongside potential risks. It can be used at the shortlist stage when the team makes its final choice and again at the planning stage. This sits alongside, but is distinct from, the need to assess the scientific rigour required. The next chapter provides more details about how they complement each other and how they can be used both for selecting topics and for planning logistics.

DOWNLOAD at www.koganpage.com/BusExp

Template – OR7. Managing risk and complexity

The pattern of risk and complexity

The template is designed to help teams to assess the level of risk that *they* perceive for their own experiment topic, but that alone is insufficient. Collectively, some teams will be risk-averse while others will be willing to push the boundaries further. That is why a comparative approach can be helpful and why even across different industries a level of benchmarking can be useful. To illustrate this, in Figure 7.1 we have plotted the seven case studies from the previous section. The two axes of the graph are the most obvious predictors of risk and complexity at the topic selection and initial planning stages:

- **X axis – stakeholders.** The main focus here is on the number of individuals or functions involved or contributing to the experiment. Internally this might include sponsors and 'gatekeepers' or whole departments, such as HR and legal. Externally it can be the number of clients, partners or regulating bodies.

- **Y axis – location.** The principal focus here is *where* the experiment is conducted. If it takes place outside of the organization, involving customers, partners or suppliers, there is immediately an increase in risk and complexity. There may also be external agencies that have an indirect influence on the experiment, such as regulators or equipment suppliers whose contribution may be limited yet important.

LOW RISK, LOW COMPLEXITY

No. 2 – Retention

No. 5 – Transparent decisions

These are categorized as low risk, low complexity because they were contained within a small part of the business and involve no external stakeholders in the experiment or control groups. The leaders of the initiative were department managers, so they were able to manage the time and resources without any reliance on other functions. The retention experiment involved two locations, but the risks were low as they were both managed by leaders in the experiment group. The external elements in both these experiments were simply

FIGURE 7.1   Choices: Risk and complexity

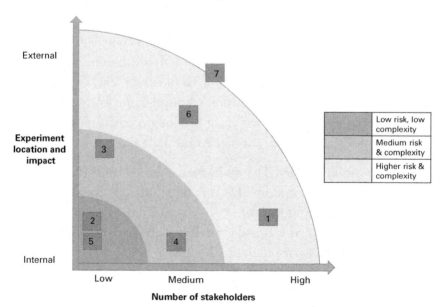

the research studies seeking ideas and solutions for their experiment. In both cases the experiments required little additional financial resources, were conducted quickly and achieved outcomes that changed organizational processes. It is these types of experiments that we recommend to newcomers.

MEDIUM RISK, MEDIUM COMPLEXITY

No. 4 – People performance

No. 3 – Sales process

The experiments here are categorized as 'medium' for different reasons. *People performance* was courageous in its hypothesis and had a reasonable level of risk since it challenged established performance management processes. Although its focus was entirely in-house, this was no guarantee of low risk. A lot of time was required to work across different functions and gain senior-level sponsorship. It also provided two useful lessons. First, it is easy to see barriers and risks where none exist; in this case the team anticipated a legal objection and were reluctant to begin the experiment until further inquiry disproved their assumptions and no such barrier existed. Second, the ability to gain 'interest' or 'acceptance' by internal stakeholders at an early stage is no guarantee that support will continue.

The *sales process* experiment is one in which the complexity and risk is reasonably contained as the experiment itself was internally managed by leaders responsible for the outcomes. Its 'medium' level of risk arose from the fact that customer involvement was required to measure the outcomes and that will always require sensitive handling. The experiment leaders had to gain buy-in from other locations, so there was additional complexity in briefing others and ensuring that the experiment and control groups were comparable and representative.

HIGH RISK, HIGH COMPLEXITY

No. 1 – 3D printing

No. 6 – Game-changing innovation

No. 7 – Pay what you want

The *3D printing* experiment was particularly bold, with a team addressing a difficult logistical and technical problem without any specialist or functional knowledge themselves. It was a good example of a problem being seen through unfamiliar eyes, but it was highly complex. The focus was on improving internal capability. The experiment was conducted entirely in-house, which explains its position on the Y axis. However, there was still a significant external component, with many barriers that risked them being unable to test their hypothesis. The team had to source the 3D equipment externally, test its technical feasibility as it had never been used in this way before, identify regulatory and quality paths with internal and external agencies, and manage client expectations.

Game-changing innovation was also bold in challenging established innovation processes and was conducted almost entirely outside the business. It was a very new idea. It meant raising $5,000 to fund the prize and getting approval from the owners of the existing processes. The team managed the complexity by partnering with a single external agency to liaise with universities across 28 countries and then sifting the ideas they received. There was a risk that the team would elicit very few responses, but they ended with a good result.

Pay what you want is also a complex and risky experiment. It involved two country locations, dozens of GPs and pharmacy staff and over 300 patients. The whole experiment was conducted externally and involved training pharmacy staff and GPs. The concept was something that had never been done in a pharmaceutical setting, so there were reputational and branding risks. In addition, getting internal approval to try the experiment was a challenge, particularly in overcoming the understandable resistance of sales directors in the experiment locations, who had one eye on meeting their current sales targets.

4. A single methodology

In addition to kickstarting a DISCOVERY mindset, the typology provides confirmation that a common approach to experimentation can be used in almost every situation. In the case of our own client workshops, often with over 20 very different topics and hypotheses, each one could be clearly assigned to one of the three categories in our typology. Yet each one was also able to use the same six-step experimentation process. In Table 7.1, the right-hand column describes that shared process. The importance of these links became clear to us when working with a global chemical business:

> We were supporting executive teams of country groups to develop experimentation as a management tool in their business area. The organization was struggling in some areas to meet short-term revenue and growth targets, and at one forum, with all the groups assembled, the CEO surprised everybody by stating: 'We've now done enough experimenting, we really need to spend our time focused on delivering our current targets.' In fairness, the CEO was doing what most others would do when faced with shareholder and analyst pressure, but they did not appreciate the impact it would have. In discussions afterwards, it was clear that the CEO's view of experimentation was focused just on the 'strategic' kind. The organization itself had just invested in an 'innovation lab' dedicated to new products and services. The CEO intended his message to mean, 'We've already got about 400 ideas in the Innovation Lab for new products and services and we don't need more. Where we do need to focus now is on the operational stuff to make sure we meet our targets.' What the assembled group *heard* was, 'Stop experimenting!!' When we explained the typology to the CEO and pointed out that the same process, behaviours and mindsets could be applied in problem-solving and performance improvement, they were better able to understand the impact of their statement. Figure 7.1 helped to explain the differences and similarities and reaffirmed that, whether focused on short-term, operational topics or longer-term, strategic issues, the same process applies. Recognizing the wider application of experimentation, the CEO became one of its strongest advocates in the company.

Summary

The main part of this chapter has provided examples of experiments across a range of situations and industries. They range from simple internal process-focused topics to complex externally focused experiments.

Our aim has been to inspire and challenge in equal measure. This comparative approach is one that we use in extending the horizons of groups we work with and why it has been chosen as a centrepiece in this chapter. We have introduced our typology to illustrate the commonality of experiments under three themes as a way of encouraging managers to learn and explore more widely. It is why we have provided guides and templates to help teams make choices to assess the level of risk they might take. It is why we have provided links to more case studies and examples that illustrate the opportunities and choices that others have made.

It means that teams can enter the EXPERIMENT phase with a final topic choice that is the result of extensive research and considered discussions.

08

Experiment process

The test of any business experiment is whether the data it produces is sufficiently reliable to make decisions with a degree of confidence.

In that sense, a simple 'try it and see' experiment can be just as valid as a more complex one if it meets that criterion. Clearly, using the same simplistic approach for a problem or opportunity that is more complex would not provide the same level of reliability or validity. In such situations a more rigorous, scientific approach is required to achieve the same level of confidence. The six-step process that we introduce in this chapter has its origins in work of Herbert Simon,[1] who sought to apply a scientific way of thinking to the art of design. Simon's methodology uses a staged, but iterative, approach to tackle complex problems and sits easily with the concepts of business experimentation. Our aim in this chapter is not just to suggest *what* to do, but also *how* you can do it. We shall propose a variety of activities, templates and questions that will provide a practical guide to experimentation.

Many 'step-by-step' guides to experimentation begin the process with the formulation of a hypothesis as though the choice of problem was clear-cut and self-evident. All too often, however, we have found in practice that too little attention is paid to the selection of a topic that is significant enough to merit experimentation. Teams leap into an experiment as though it were a pre-ordained project. By contrast, the six-step process places considerable emphasis on the pre-hypothesis stage to ensure that:

- The topic selected has the potential to add measurable business value.
- The choice of topic is the result of a rigorous, criteria-led selection process.
- The problem or opportunity is extensively researched to:
  - justify the assumptions being made;
  - gain stakeholder perspectives on the topic and its impact on them;
  - identify other variables or influences that may require isolation.
- Testing the hypothesis is practical and the outcomes are realistic, measurable and verifiable.

We will describe each stage of the process in turn (starting with IDENTIFY), but the sequence is not meant to be set in concrete. In practice, the process is more iterative, going back and forth as new information is gained. Often the stages will overlap or run concurrently. This becomes particularly relevant in the early phases when the problem or opportunity is being researched, different solutions are being considered, and the hypothesis is being developed.

Setting the scene

The six-step process has been designed to be suitable for a wide variety of experiments. It can be used in new ventures as successfully as in large established corporations. It is equally suitable for entrepreneurs and executives. In this chapter we have chosen to use quite a complex setting as the main exemplar, if only to provide practical insights for the more demanding situations. In doing so, our aim is that others with simpler experiments will be able to adapt each step as necessary while continuing to follow the same process.

The situation that we have chosen to act as an exemplar has the following features:

- a large organization with multiple locations and group functions;
- an experimental team of four to six managers from the same or different business functions;
- an experiment is supported either formally, as part of a corporate initiative, or informally and spontaneously by a team that wishes to become 'more innovative';
- an experiment with the potential to add significant value to the business;
- a timeframe of three to six months for the conduct of the experiment.

The experiment process – overview and narrative

We shall describe in detail how an experiment group, similar to our exemplar, can apply the six-step process. The illustration and the notes below provide an overview of the methodology.

We begin with IDENTIFY, given that our choice of exemplar is part of an organizational initiative requiring the experiment team to research topic choices and select a shortlist that will meet a set of criteria.

Moving to the DISCOVER phase, the team is expected to explore the shortlist options to get 'under the skin' of the problem or opportunity. This will overlap with the IDEATE phase, as the team begins to research new ideas and create choices for hypothetical solutions.

Armed with a shortlist of fully researched topics, the DEFINE phase requires the team to make their choices: first, about which topic will be selected for experimentation and, second, which interventions may be used as solutions. This then forms the basis of the hypothesis.

The EXPERIMENT phase concerns the testing of the hypothesis and how the experiment needs to be designed to yield a robust result. There are many factors to be considered here as the team balances

the need for scientific rigour against the practical and logistical challenges of people and project management.

The EVALUATION phase is the stage at which the team collates
and analyses the results of the experiment to gain insights and
make recommendations that will be dependent upon the robust-
ness of the findings. The evaluation phase is also an opportunity
to share learning.

FIGURE 8.1   A process for experimentation

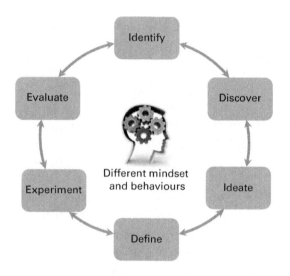

IDENTIFY ➔ Identify the problems, opportunities or gaps you want to
address.

DISCOVER ➔ Research and explore the problem or opportunity – internally
and externally.

IDEATE ➜ Widen the scope to seek new ideas for potential solutions and hypotheses.

DEFINE ➜ Formulate the hypothesis and define the measurability of the outcomes.

EXPERIMENT ➜ Lay out the practicalities of running the experiment and testing the hypothesis.

EVALUATE ➜ Analyse and interpret the results. Recommend actions and next steps.

Identify

Identify the problems, opportunities or gaps you want to address

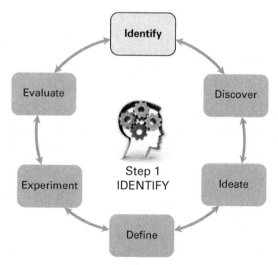

In many cases the problem or opportunity for experimentation may well have identified itself – this may be an obvious new challenge emerging or an ongoing problem that has not been resolved by traditional methods. On other occasions, experimentation may be conducted by organizational teams as part of a wider initiative, by individual managers with their direct reports or by small business owners. Driven by a fast-moving competitive environment, they seek new ways of doing things and want to encourage a more innovative approach to the way they deliver services or products. This opens up a vast array of opportunities, and one of the easier tasks in the experimentation process is identifying problems that need solving or processes that need fixing or opportunities that need capturing. Put a group of managers or employees in a room and, whether it is a guided process using hackathons and scrums or simply providing a flipchart to share ideas, the results will almost always be copious.

We recently joined a group of six UK banking executives just one hour after they started their 'identify' discussions and found two large whiteboards crammed with over 40 ideas for experiments. They had prepared for the session, using a tailored questionnaire. The outcomes were exactly as we had hoped. The session had been punchy and fast-paced, and the team did well to get so many ideas 'on the board'. They had avoided the temptation to discuss the merits or flaws of each idea as they emerged and simply charted everything without discussion. As we praised them for their productivity, it was clear that their success had also raised a number of concerns. Omar, a managing director in the investment bank, shared the team's disquiet:

> Okay, some of these ideas are a bit whacky and some may well be too much to bite off, but that still leaves us with about 20 pretty bold and 'doable' possibilities that all seem to be important. How the heck are we going to shortlist this lot?

If capturing ideas is the easy part, one of the most difficult tasks is prioritizing the list and selecting the 'right' topic(s) for experimentation.

Generating ideas

Ask a manager or management team about things that could be done better in their business and there will be plenty of suggestions. From an experiment perspective, those ideas should, of course, be taken into account, but they may not always provide the whole picture. They are often derived from a narrow perspective on the business and sometimes fail to look beyond functional viewpoints or the most obvious organizational challenges. Where they are chosen by an individual or a small cohort rather than the whole experiment group, that too can narrow the options. Experimentation is about expanding horizons, and it is for these reasons that we encourage clients to use techniques and activities in the IDENTIFY stage that will build on their early ideas.

This becomes particularly relevant for teams that have already decided on a single experiment idea or have shortlisted two or three topics at the outset. What can appear to be a decisive start does not necessarily lead to a positive outcome. Our role in such cases is not to dissuade teams from their original choice. The final topic choice in an experiment will always reside with the team itself. However, we do need to ensure that their final selection is based on a level of scrutiny and rigour that would normally have been applied had they begun with a wider range of topics.

It is obvious that generating even more ideas will take time, but this is not just about providing comparators or promoting a more detailed examination of the original choice. While they are important factors, a less obvious reason is that the IDENTIFY phase is the first time that the team will be working together as a unit and it sets the scene for how they will work collectively as the experiment progresses. Creating a more collaborative approach to decision-making at this stage encourages everyone to share their ideas and be involved in the discussion. Even if the team returns to their original set of options, the time spent will have added new perspectives and created a greater sense of ownership among its members.

There are countless techniques for encouraging ideas, but our focus in the IDENTIFY stage is to generate topics for experimentation that have real business significance. We want to encourage workshop discussion about problems and possibilities faced by the group that have the potential to add value. The following are the most effective techniques that we have used for these types of discussion:

ACTIVITY 1: TAILORED QUESTIONNAIRES

These are designed to be completed individually prior to a workshop. They are ideal for setting up a discussion to prioritize the initial topic choices. In the downloadable guides, they are tailored for the following: the organizational team and SMEs.

DOWNLOAD at www.koganpage.com/BusExp

Guides – Opportunities for experimentation in large organizations (OR1) and Opportunities for experimentation in SMEs (OR1a)

ACTIVITY 2: SWOT OR PESTLE DISCUSSION FORUMS

These are well-known techniques that remain a powerful vehicle for generating discussions and sharing perspectives when used in a workshop setting. Both have relevance to teams at different levels, but PESTLE is more appropriate for those more closely influenced by the external environment. They are equally suited to small business owners and executive teams in larger organizations.

DOWNLOAD at www.koganpage.com/BusExp

Guides – How to run a SWOT–PESTLE workshop in organizations (OR2) and SMEs (OR2a)

Filtering and prioritizing

Let's return to our group of banking executives with their concerns about shortlisting the 40 ideas that they had generated. Their first inclination was to reduce the list by eliminating the 'whacky' ones and others that seemed too ambitious. It is an error made by many teams. Dismissing half of the topics in one fell swoop negates the creative effort that went into generating the ideas. Apart from discarding opportunities with potential, it may also disenfranchise those who contributed them. As an alternative we suggest that the process can be made more inclusive and collaborative if it uses a series of 'gateways' to filter and prioritize the options.

GATEWAY 1: AFFINITY AND CLUSTER GROUPS

Using an affinity diagram is one way of grouping seemingly disparate ideas by similarity of theme. This is what we recommended to the team of banking executives. The process also encourages a group to depart from their habitual style of thinking and move beyond preconceived categories. The executives used the process described in the box overleaf (Activity 3: Affinity and cluster groups).

ACTIVITY 3: AFFINITY AND CLUSTER GROUPS

1   All the topics are written on sticky notes and posted on a board.

2   Without identifying any headings and *without any conversation*, the team simultaneously move the notes into related groupings:

   o   If a topic fits two headings, an additional note is used.

   o   It is okay to move a note that someone else has placed.

   o   A separate area is created for 'miscellaneous' topics that don't fit easily into any category.

   o   Topics are not ordered or prioritized – they are simply grouped.

   o   The number of category groups should set at between five and eight.

3   Once all the sticky notes have been clustered, the team agrees on a heading for each cluster.

4   Once completed, the team members discuss their rationale, both for their choice of topics and their choice of clusters.

5   The team then work together to continue moving the sticky notes until they all agree on the clusters, the headings and the topics under each.

6   The team then prioritize the topics in each cluster according to the twin criteria of business value and enthusiasm for the topic.

7   The final headings should be determined by the team, but as a guide, some of the headings that often emerge are:

   o   products and services;

   o   people;

   o   profitability – revenue and costs;

   o   processes, structures and systems;

   o   performance;

   o   productivity.

Using the activity described above, the banking team reduced their original 40 ideas to a more realistic choice of 14 in under 2 hours. One of the ideas they had considered 'whacky' had been embraced within another topic and two of the ideas they had considered too ambitious were retained to explore ways of managing their

FIGURE 8.2   Affinity and cluster diagrams

Products	People	Profitability	Processes	Productivity	Performance
Idea	Idea	Idea	Idea	Idea	Idea
Idea	Idea	Idea	Idea	Idea	Idea
Idea	Idea	Idea	Idea	Idea	Idea
Idea	Idea	Idea	Idea	Idea	Idea
Idea	Idea	Idea		Idea	
Idea	Idea				
Idea	Idea				

From this...   ... to this

scope. The team agreed that the activity had benefited the way that they worked together by raising the level of discussion and encouraging different perspectives. However, the added enthusiasm brought its own challenges as the team became concerned about how they were going to further shortlist the remaining topics, all of which were credible options, to a much smaller number. They wanted to continue the collective approach but with a decision based on rationality rather than individual preference or emotional attachment. We encouraged them to continue with the gateway approach to refine their choices further. The following section illustrates how this was achieved.

DOWNLOAD at www.koganpage.com/BusExp

Guide – OR5. Filtering and prioritizing ideas

GATEWAY 2: TOPIC CHOICE CRITERIA

The team of six was split into two groups and each trio was assigned seven topic ideas. Individually at first, and then as a trio, the groups scored each topic idea against a set of criteria. The criteria had been selected by the team and Table 8.1 provides a typical criteria example.

TABLE 8.1   Criteria for shortlisting experiment ideas

Experiment topic 1: Describe the problem/opportunity	Score 1–10
Scope – The scope of the topic, and the expected geographical locations and timelines, are manageable.	
Strategic – This experiment idea will address a problem or opportunity that will contribute directly to our business ambitions.	
Value-add – This experiment idea will provide *measurable* benefits that will contribute to business performance.	
Experimental approach? – This experiment is bold and courageous. It explores fresh perspectives, looks at new ideas and will challenge current thinking.	
Passion – This is a topic that energizes and excites the team.	

ACTIVITY 4: SHORTLISTING AGAINST CRITERIA

1   This activity is designed to create a framework for discussion rather than a pure numerical assessment and should take less than two hours.

2   Each trio discusses how they have attributed their scores and agrees a priority order for their experiment ideas.

3   With the whole group together, they agree three topics as a shortlist and prepare to move to the DISCOVER stage.

4   At this point the team is asked to record the five 'runners up' in the filtering process so as not to forget them.

DOWNLOAD at www.koganpage.com/BusExp

Guide – OR8. Topic selection criteria

Some of our corporate client programmes have involved hundreds of senior managers working in experiment teams over the course of a few years. Asking teams to record their top 8 or 10 topics produces a valuable 'back catalogue' of problems and opportunities deemed to be important. It can act as a window onto the true issues facing the organization, whether or not they were chosen for experimentation.

Discover

Research and explore the problem or opportunity – internally and externally

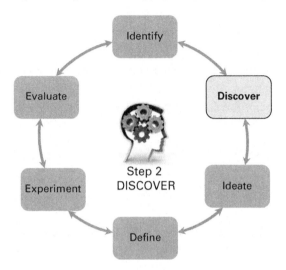

As the experiment topic selection is distilled to a shortlist, we move to the DISCOVER phase in the six-step process. It involves two distinct elements:

Understanding the problem

One of the main tenets of Herbert Simon's methodology is that it is vitally important to gain a deep understanding of the problem to be addressed by the experiment and its significance on stakeholders. After shortlisting a few topic ideas, too often we see experiment teams jump to their favoured topic. Partly driven by the desire to get going and partly fixated on symptoms rather than underlying causes, they can easily embark on the wrong experiment. This is not about slowing things down but about ensuring that each idea is thought through sufficiently to make a carefully considered choice.

One example of good practice in this area is the USA West Coast HR organization that we highlighted in Chapter 7. Taking time to get underneath the problem of staff retention, they found that the real issue was limited to a very specific subset of employees. They had between one and two years' service and were extremely productive. Yet their turnover at nearly 60 per cent was twice the average. Surveying this group further, they discovered that almost 70 per cent of departures were avoidable. These two pieces of information changed the whole focus of their experiment and helped them to select the most impactful interventions for that particular group. The results from this experiment showed the benefits of taking time in the discovery phase and yielded impressive increases in the rates of retention in their main locations.

Explore solutions

Having gained greater clarity around the problem or opportunity, the second part of the DISCOVER phase is researching how others have addressed the topic. It is here that we once again encourage teams to look beyond their own business function. The 'external' view includes looking across organizational boundaries as well as beyond the business itself. The 10-question checklist in Table 8.2 provides a starting point for teams in this part of the DISCOVER phase. It is not meant to be exhaustive and teams will benefit by tailoring it to their own circumstances. Most teams find that dividing the responsibilities for investigating specific sources of information is the best use of time at this stage. They then share their findings as a group and record them for later use. As teams undertake the DISCOVER phase, they not only create a better understanding of the problem/opportunity, but also uncover potential ideas and solutions for the IDEATE phase that follows.

TABLE 8.2   10 Discover questions – sample checklist

1	Internal stakeholders	What are their views about this problem or opportunity? How is it impacting them? How might it benefit them?
2	Assumptions	What are the assumptions you are making about the problem or opportunity? Who can help to provide clarity about their validity?
3	Organization	What are others doing *currently* in your organization about this problem/opportunity?
4	Organization	What has been done *historically* in your organization that might influence the topic?
5	Your industry	What does research say about how this topic is being addressed in your *industry*?
6	Other industries	What are 'leading' organizations in other industries doing that may have similar issues?
7	Competition	What do you know about how your competitors are dealing with this topic?
8	External stakeholders	What exactly are customers/suppliers/partners/investors saying about this? How can you find out more?
9	Professional bodies	What can you learn from professional bodies or research institutes about the topic?
10	Academia and research	What does the latest research tell you about the topic? What research papers provide different perspectives?

3

Ideate

Widen the scope to seek new ideas for potential solutions and hypotheses

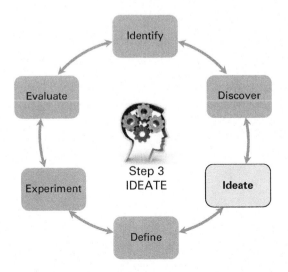

This part of the process is about ideas-generation. Mentally it means teams 'going wide' in terms of possible solutions. The research that uncovered options during the DISCOVER phase will often be a starting point. As teams explore and learn about ways in which others have addressed the topic, it can spark ideas and a curiosity about how the interventions might be adapted to their own situation. The DISCOVER and IDEATION phases are iterative and often overlap. Some ideas from the earlier phases become short-lived and others may be built upon in the IDEATION phase. Too often we see teams stop at this point to concentrate on the potential interventions already on the table. But the ideation phase is about *divergent* thinking so as to embrace even more ideas and innovative solutions and not converge too early. The point here is that earlier ideas emerging from the DISCOVER phase will have been generated by those *already* familiar with the problem or opportunity – such as customers, competitors, professional bodies and academia. These insights are crucial in understanding the problem/opportunity, testing out early assumptions and gaining new ideas based on previous experiences.

However, as important as they are, they can be limiting in terms of divergent thinking. Henry Ford was reported to have said, 'If I ask my customers what they wanted, they'd have said a "faster horse" and the motor car would not have been born.' It becomes important therefore that in this phase the team engages others with very different perspectives as well as those who may be totally new to the topic. The purpose is to expand their horizons of thought and generate even more ideas.

While we emphasize the iterative nature of the DISCOVER and IDEATE phases, it is worth pointing out the difference:

- DISCOVER is primarily about exploring the *problem/opportunity* to understand the issue in greater breadth and depth and how others have addressed it.

- IDEATE is about a totally *fresh perspective.* Here we see teams allowing their imagination to run riot and explore completely new ideas.

The aim at the end of the IDEATE stage is to reveal a range of potential *solutions* to the problem or different ways in which the opportunity may be exploited. It is the ideas that emerge from this phase that will be considered as interventions in the experiment itself. There are many activities to help the process, and the following downloadable guide provides an activity to support the ideation phase.

DOWNLOAD at www.koganpage.com/BusExp

Guide – OR4. Ideation (freethinking)

4

Define

Formulate the hypothesis and define the measurability of the outcomes

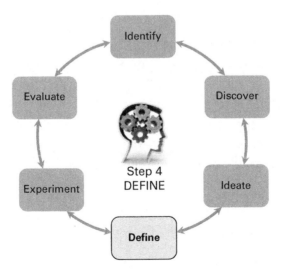

The DEFINE stage has two elements. First, it is the final convergent phase as the team reduces its shortlist to a single topic. Second, it is where the team finalizes a verifiable and measurable hypothesis that will drive the experiment.

Let's return to our banking executives. At the start of the DEFINE stage the team had spent a total of three days together over a four-week period that enabled them to:

- Produce 40 topic ideas as a result of individual inputs and workshop discussions.
- Filter the ideas through two selection gateways to produce a shortlist of three topics.
- Assess the business potential of each topic.
- Formulate a working hypothesis for each of the shortlisted topics.
- Explore the shortlist to gain further insights into the problem or opportunity.
- Use the DISCOVER questionnaire.
- Use the 'Ideate Activity' to share findings and produce even more ideas for ways of testing the working hypotheses.

The task now is to select one topic from the shortlist.

Final gateway

The DEFINE stage means becoming even more practical and realistic as the final selection is made. It means making decisions about the manageability of the topic, assessing the risks and considering issues of complexity and scope. At this point there is often one topic that stands out as an obvious choice, particularly after the DISCOVER and IDEATE stages have created additional insights. Armed with all this information, the teams will begin to make their final choice and it is here that we return to the question, 'How scientific is scientific?' We pay more attention to this question in the EXPERIMENT phase, but at this stage, we expect teams to start considering the risk and complexity of each topic and the rigour required as they make their final selection.

Developing the hypothesis

WHAT IS A HYPOTHESIS?

In many ways a hypothesis might be seen as a prediction, but it is much more than a guess. As Figure 8.3 illustrates, it is informed by a deep understanding of the problem or opportunity that is followed by an exploration of potential solutions.

A hypothesis then is 'a precise, testable statement that proposes a solution to a problem where the specific outcome is anticipated but uncertain'.

A testable hypothesis is a conjecture that can be proved or disproved as a result of experimentation, data collection or experience. It may be considered a reflection of a team's expectations, but the point of the experiment is to determine whether the statement is true or not. A disproven hypothesis can be just as valuable if it provides robust data on which future decisions can be based.

In a business experiment, teams often fall into the trap of creating a hypothesis early in the process and rarely referring to it again. As we will see later, the hypothesis is one of the most important tools of an experiment. It should be a constant reference point. It is fundamental to how the experiment will be set up, how its progress is monitored and how the results are evaluated. In a car it is the equivalent of the satellite navigation providing direction, the speedometer, odometer and fuel gauge monitoring the journey, and the warning systems alerting the driver of potential hazards.

FIGURE 8.3 A process for experimentation

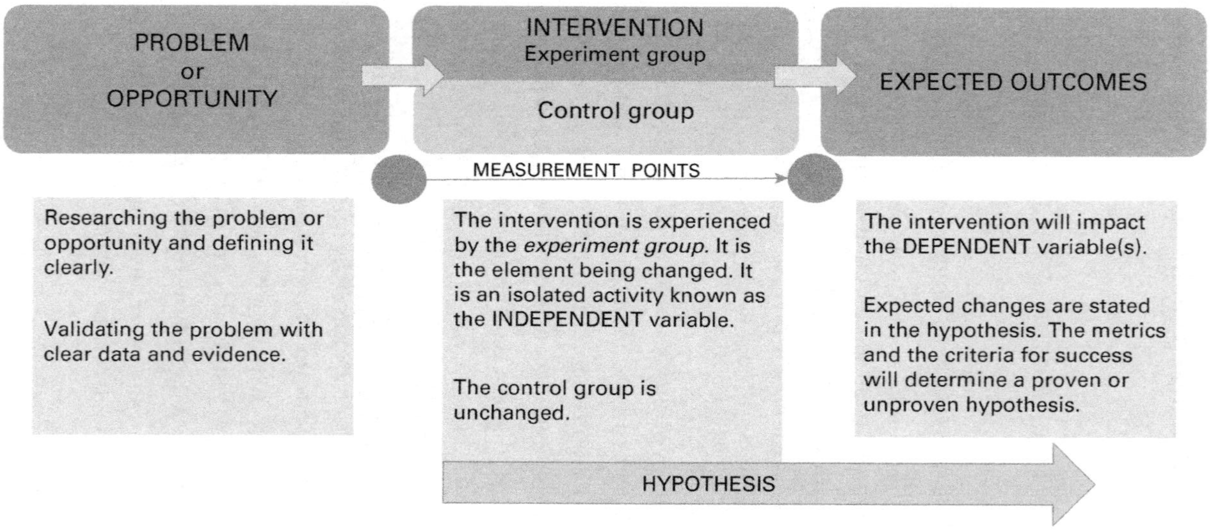

PROBLEM or OPPORTUNITY

Researching the problem or opportunity and defining it clearly.

Validating the problem with clear data and evidence.

INTERVENTION
Experiment group

Control group

MEASUREMENT POINTS

The intervention is experienced by the *experiment group*. It is the element being changed. It is an isolated activity known as the INDEPENDENT variable.

The control group is unchanged.

EXPECTED OUTCOMES

The intervention will impact the DEPENDENT variable(s).

Expected changes are stated in the hypothesis. The metrics and the criteria for success will determine a proven or unproven hypothesis.

HYPOTHESIS

Writing a hypothesis

We ask clients to write their hypotheses in a relatively simple way. By the DEFINE stage they are already very familiar with the problem, so we concentrate on the possible solution and expected outcomes in the following format:

If we do X, then we will achieve Y.

X is the independent variable. This is the selected *single* intervention or the element that will be changed for the experiment. It is assumed to have a direct effect on the outcome – the dependent variable.

Y is the dependent variable and is the expected outcome that will be measured.

We describe two examples of hypotheses in the examples below and, while they may appear to be uncomplicated statements, they are more intricate in their construction. We expect the hypothesis statement to be a portal that uncovers *exactly* what is happening in an experiment.

EXAMPLE 1

Problem. An international recruitment firm based in Australia recognized a lack of 'strategic' oversight with regard to their largest client, a global online retailer. They were operating out of four offices, separately located, each one serving a separate part of the client's business. They were missing synergies and this was resulting in poor coordination and reduced productivity. With each location managing its own client relationships, it also restricted opportunities for cross-selling. The recruitment firm preferred a 'partnership' arrangement with key clients as they considered it better value for the client, but relationships were not at a senior level and most interactions were transactional. The team researched the problem both internally and with the client and developed this initial hypothesis:

If we create *a centralized account management system* for client A, then we will **improve strategic oversight**.

This works fine as a headline hypothesis but prompts many questions. It demands a deeper level of interrogation. When the team were asked to be more specific about the outcomes, their hypothesis was expanded. As an example, and taking the dependent variable of 'strategic oversight', the Y part of the hypothesis became:

> If we create *a centralized account management system* for client A, then we will **enhance client satisfaction, improve productivity and increase EBITA**.

This only provides a part of the interrogation as each development of the hypothesis should raise another level of questions: What do we mean by 'productivity'? Do we have base measures in place to evaluate the changes in client satisfaction? By how much do we expect to increase EBITA?

The same type of interrogation is appropriate for the X element (the intervention) of the hypothesis: What do we really mean by a centralized account management system? How do we fit this with existing systems?

As the interrogation of the hypothesis continues, it produces the basis of the experiment plan.

EXAMPLE 2

Problem. This chemical firm based in Germany was finding it increasingly difficult to attract graduates in a diminishing talent pool. There were particular shortages of engineering candidates and a study indicated that over 90 per cent of those interviewed did not see the company as a 'preferred employer'. The company was using a standard job template that was not tailored to specific professions or target groups. The experiment team decided to try a relatively simple experiment. Based on the feedback from their research of the problem, they produced a small number of tailored advertisements to compare with the standard advertisement (as the control) using the same job portal. Their hypothesis was:

> By *tailoring job adverts to the needs of specific target groups* we will **increase the attraction rate and the number and quality of applications**.

In each hypothesis statement the italicised text is X and the text in bold is Y.

We will see in the next section how the two experiment teams made their choices about the experiment process.

Experiment

Lay out the practicalities of running the experiment and testing the hypothesis

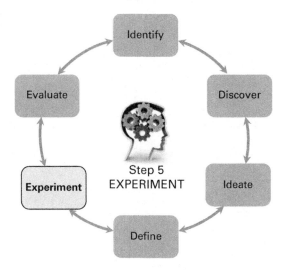

Let's start where we left off... the hypothesis statement. We highlighted how a simple sentence can be interrogated to become the starting point for the design of the experiment and then as a guide to monitor the whole process. In Figure 8.4 we use the hypothesis of the Australian recruiter as an example. It shows just a small sample of questions, challenges and choices that the team needs to consider as they interrogate each word of the hypothesis. The answers to the questions will provide the foundation for the design of the experiment.

FIGURE 8.4 The hypothesis as a portal

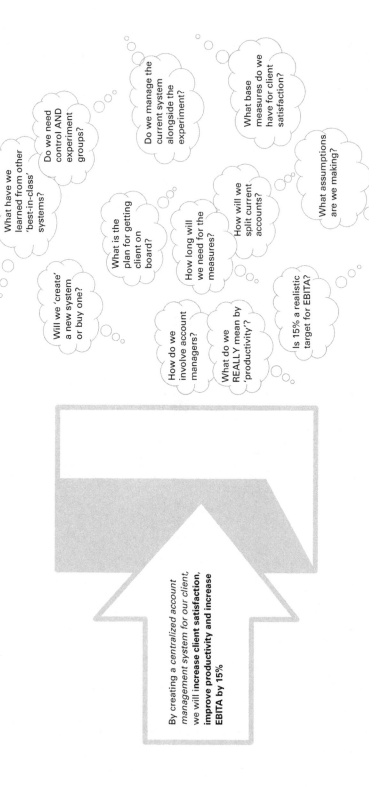

This section is aimed at answering many of the questions that emerge when teams prepare for the EXPERIMENT phase. People want to get a better feel for the following choices:

1 *What are the best experiment design choices for testing our hypothesis?*
2 *What will be the practical and logistical considerations?*
3 *How do we assess the amount of scientific rigour needed?*
4 *How do we manage and monitor the process as a team?*
5 *What do the most successful teams do? How do they avoid the pitfalls?*

Q1. What are the experiment design choices?

It will be evident from the examples so far that a business experiment can take many forms. The earlier phases will influence the decision about the experiment design, but there can still be choices to be made even at the hypothesis stage. With the Australian recruiters, the team had to decide how they would compare the new centralized account management system with the existing process. Which experiment design would be most effective in testing their hypothesis? In this case they decided that an approach that required a split sample of control group and an experiment group was impractical. After all, they were testing a centralized system, so splitting it in two made no sense and it would also dilute the sample sizes. They decided to test the intervention with the whole account management group and used historical data from the previous arrangement as their comparison. Rather than an A/B test, it was a pre-/post-test.

In the other example of the German team exploring better ways to attract talent, they did use an experiment and control group approach. In this situation it was not a 'group' but a way of comparing the existing style of advertising (control) with the new tailored version (experiment). In their case the comparability was perfect as they used the same job portal to test the attractiveness of the advertising aimed at exactly the same target group. The result over a four-week period was that experiment group advertisements increased applications fourfold and the quality of the applicants was much higher.

Appendix A provides more detail about the different types of experiment, with examples. Here are four classic types.

A. RANDOMIZED CONTROL TRIALS (AND A/B TESTING)

A/B testing is probably the most common form of experimentation in business and became popular with web designers and analysts at the turn of the millennium. It is this more robust type of business experiment design that features in most of our examples.

B. MULTIVARIATE TESTING (MVT)

Multivariate testing has similar characteristics to A/B or RCT testing, but in this case there are multiple dependent variables. For example, it might take the form, A/B1, B2, B3 where the experiment or treatment groups (B) are tested with three different versions of the intervention.

C. PROOF OF CONCEPT

Concept testing or 'proof of principle' can be a very simple experiment to measure initial customer reactions to a service or product without actually producing the product. It is widely used in marketing but can also be used in testing business models, pricing, promotions and customer experience.

D. PILOTS, PROTOTYPES, MINIMUM VIABLE PRODUCTS (MVPS) AND MOCK-UPS

The proof of concept is aimed at testing an idea, whereas the four types of experiments we consider here are, in most cases, dealing with a *tangible* product or service. In each case the experiment aim is to present a 'taster' of the final version that can be developed using feedback loops from customers and end users.

The design choices here are offered as the most common examples of business experiments that we encounter. Most of the experiments we describe in this book fit into the earlier categories of random control trials (RCT), multivariate trials (MVT) and concept testing. The descriptions in the next sections relate primarily to these types of experiments.

Q2. What are the practical and logistics options?

The questions we expect teams to be addressing in the early stages of the EXPERIMENT phase will be about *how* they test the hypothesis in a practical sense. Every experiment will have its own set of circumstances. We ask teams to begin framing their plan around the *who, where and when* of the experiment and how they *manage the scope and complexity*.

FIGURE 8.5 Experiment plan

We shall take each in turn.

A. WHO?

Most experiments involve four distinct groups of people critical to its success:

1 The most important will be those actually involved in the control and experiment groups. If an experiment is expected to be scalable across the organization, those chosen as the experiment and control groups need to be representative of the wider population.

A simple test for the team, once the experiment and control groups are selected, is to determine whether a repeated test with different groups would be expected to produce the same outcome.

2 There is a 'hidden' group that experiment teams can often overlook. Whenever an experiment is undertaken in any size of organization, there will be people on the periphery. This becomes particularly important when that group may also be affected or even threatened by the outcomes of the experiment. Experimentation is not a change initiative, but there is a responsibility to manage possible disruptive elements by considering the peripheral stakeholders and their communication needs.

3 *Internal stakeholders.* We recommend that teams produce a stakeholder map and a communication plan in the early stages and review it regularly. This will highlight the needs of the 'hidden' group but also identify additional key players in the experiment. These might include legal, IT or HR functions or individuals whose 'permission' is needed. This might also include sales directors or country managers where the experiment is taking place. Another important internal stakeholder if the experiment is in a large organization is the 'sponsor'. This will be someone who has a vested interest in the outcomes of the experiment and who can act as a coach and 'client'.

4 *External stakeholders.* If an experiment is externally focused, the most obvious and important group will be the clients or customers who stand to gain from it. In our experience, customers are usually pleased to be involved since, if the experiment yields a result, they will be the main beneficiary. Other external stakeholders include those individuals, research groups or professional bodies that were involved in the DISCOVER and IDEATE phases and may still have a stake in the experiment.

Taking time early in an experiment to draw up a stakeholder map and communication plan is time well spent. Frequently updating it and agreeing actions as a group is equally important.

B. WHERE?

The location of an experiment is often dictated by the hypothesis. In a large organization there may be more options but, by the time the team has gone through the early stages of the experiment, the choice will be narrowed. In a small business with fewer locations, there is already a limited choice. The team will know best where to test their hypothesis, but we do urge some caution. The main consideration in the 'where?' question is the comparability of locations.

In an experiment we are always aiming to compare 'like with like'. Running a sales experiment with the control group in one location and an experiment group in another, where the locations differ significantly in their consumer profiles or market buoyancy, is not a fair test of the hypothesis. Even localized issues can influence results. A supermarket chain in the USA was concerned about its retention and engagement scores. It decided to run an experiment that they hoped would create an improvement in employee satisfaction. They selected two stores that were comparable in terms of revenue, customer profile and retention rate. The outcome of the experiment was that the retention scores in the experiment group had deteriorated. Upon investigation, the team discovered that, during the course of the experiment's four-month run, a rival supermarket had increased its hourly wage by 50 cents. This is an example of an extraneous variable that had not been factored into the results. It had clearly skewed the retention rates as supermarket employees sought to make an extra $20 a week one block away.

C. WHEN AND HOW LONG?

We mentioned earlier that many experiments will be simple, short, sharp interventions with a rapid feedback loop. The experiments we describe in this book are invariably more complex and take longer to conduct. As such, the timing question is less about when to start and more about when to stop. The duration of the experiment is dependent on two things. First, the experiment needs to run long enough for statistically significant data to be gathered. Second, it needs to run long enough for comparisons between the experiment and control groups to be reliable. As an example, an experiment may be testing a new sales process but would need to run for a whole three-month sales cycle to provide a fair comparison with the existing process. Similarly, changes to an annual performance management system may need to run concurrently with the existing process. In cases where the experiment is testing *behavioural* change, the duration of the intervention will need to be long enough for the changes to be reliably detected and measured.

Many experiments manage issues of timing and scope by phasing the test. One US group that wanted to test new recruitment and onboarding processes to improve employee retention split the experiment into two phases. The first phase focused on ways of increasing the number of applicants and the second phase built upon it by testing different induction techniques for enhancing engagement.

D. MANAGING SCOPE AND COMPLEXITY

In the previous chapter we plotted a number of experiments on a chart to illustrate the level of risk and complexity. We introduced the following template at the final topic selection stages but also stressed the importance of revisiting it at the experiment planning stage. It is separate, yet complementary, to the scientific assessment in the next section, but both will inform the responses to the who, what, when questions above and be integral to the way in which the risks and the experiment itself are managed.

DOWNLOAD at www.koganpage.com/BusExp

Template – OR7. Managing risk and complexity

Q3. How scientific do we need to be?

Managers instinctively understand that business experimentation is an economic activity and not a scientific one. They accept that greater complexity demands greater scientific rigour, yet they still seek guidance about the level of thoroughness. When answering the question in the title in the early stages of an experiment, we use the statement below as a starting point:

An experiment needs to be scientific enough to produce robust data that can support managerial decisions with a reasonable degree of confidence.

It is generic for two reasons. First, every experiment situation is different and there can be no single answer. It means that experiment teams have to interrogate the statement and produce answers that are relevant to *their* experiment. Second, the level of rigour cannot be confidently assessed until the hypothesis has been formulated.

Now, as the experiment begins, there needs to be a focus on how the chosen topic and its hypothesis will be tested. More detailed planning is required, and we expect teams to revisit the statement with much greater precision. It is here that we break down the statement into its component parts to provide additional guidance.

'SCIENTIFIC ENOUGH'?

Sometimes, the experiment topic clearly requires a process of strict control of the variables, sample sizes and control/experiment groups from the outset. On other occasions such controls may be less important, particularly if the 'experiment' is in the 'let's try it and see what happens' category. To complicate things further, an experiment can often increase in complexity as part of a phased approach. By starting small, building on the information gained and re-testing on a grander scale, the demand for a more scientific approach will almost certainly increase as the complexity increases. So how do teams make these types of decisions as they plan the practicalities of their experiments?

Table 8.3 offers some answers. It is neither prescriptive nor exhaustive and we expect teams to tailor it to their own situations, selecting those elements that are most important for ensuring the validity of their experiment. A template and a description of how to get the best from the process are provided as downloadable guides.

TABLE 8.3   How scientific is scientific?

Experimental elements	Level of importance	Level of confidence	Actions required
Control and experiment groups are directly comparable apart from the independent variable(s)			
Controls are in place to manage potential cross-contamination between control and experiment groups that can influence results			
Extraneous variables are identified and their potential influence managed			
Sample sizes are large enough to be statistically significant and to enable extrapolation to a larger population if required			
The experiment duration is sufficient to achieve meaningful measurements			
Experiment timing is relevant to business cadence – eg budget or sales cycles			
The scope of the experiment is manageable within the expected timeframe			
Geographical and cultural dimensions that could influence the results have been considered			
Accurate measures are in place at the baseline and to record outcomes to provide a robust test of the hypothesis (qualitative and quantitative?)			
Consideration has been given to Hawthorne and John Henry effects			

Level of importance – a score of 1–5, where level 5 means that the element is critical to achieving experiment outcomes
Level of confidence – a score of 1–5, where level 5 means that there is full confidence in that element being managed
Actions required – where there is a negative gap between the two columns, what needs to happen?

DOWNLOAD at www.koganpage.com/BusExp

Template and guide – OR9. Assessing scientific rigour

'ROBUST DATA'?

The same activity (or a revised template) can be used as the experiment progresses to become part of the monitoring and control processes. The aim here is to encourage teams to take stock at regular intervals to ensure that the data being gathered is accurate, sufficient and remains relevant for testing the hypothesis. Business experiments rarely go to plan, so it is vital to keep tabs on the continuing validity and reliability of the information emanating from the experiment. For example, we often see opportunities for teams to add to the original measures as the experiment progresses and as it uncovers new sources of information. The types of questions we would expect to emerge from discussions as teams monitor progress include:

- Are we confident that our baseline data is accurate and remains relevant?
- Are the sample sizes large enough to be statistically significant?
- Is there a danger that the results are systemically biased?
- Is the information we are gathering sufficient to test the hypothesis?
- What secondary findings (unplanned) can we draw from the experiment?
- Are there better ways for capturing the qualitative information?
- Do we need more time?

'DECISIONS WITH A REASONABLE DEGREE OF CONFIDENCE'

We suggested in the previous chapter that experimentation need not always conform to a perfect 'gold standard' process. Yet our clients instinctively strive to achieve perfection by assimilating as much information as possible. This is perfectly understandable but, in an experimental setting, it can be counterproductive and is one of the adjustments to attitudes that needs to be made. The benefits of more data for making better decisions need to be balanced with the time and costs associated with extending the experiment. In the same way that teams need to become comfortable with uncertainty and ambiguity as they adopt an experimental mindset, so they also need to accept that all business decisions involve some degree of risk. It may be counterintuitive to be willing to accept only a 'reasonable' degree of confidence in an experimentally driven decision, but this is in the nature of experimentation.

Q4. Working effectively as a team?

As the experiment gets under way, there is a tendency for groups to revert to 'project' mode as they take more control of the process. Project management skills take on greater relevance at this stage, but it is important that this frame of mind does not impair or replace an experimental mindset. This means managing the process while also maintaining a sense of curiosity. It means continuing to question whether the experiment is delivering the results required to reliably test the hypothesis. There are a number of activities that we would expect during the early EXPERIMENT phase that enables the team to preserve a balance between the scientific rigour and the logistical aspects of the experiment.

A. TEAM DYNAMICS AND LEADERSHIP

Experiment teams come in many forms. Some will be an intact team with an existing hierarchy, some are formed from a peer group and others might be a cadre of people in a small business. Whatever the construct, a team will need to decide how it works together and how it manages the experiment process, even if it is already an existing team. There are the obvious 'hygiene' factors of location, frequency and duration of meetings, but there are more complex factors to consider. Where experiments are additional to the 'day job', scheduled meetings can often be ineffectual. In these situations, meetings can become general updates with too little attention being paid to issues that matter and as individual team members struggle to balance their work priorities with their experimental commitments. Additionally, there is the question of team leadership. When working with peer groups we have found that for some it is beneficial to dispense with a leader. Others may prefer to adopt a leader as a facilitator to help with decision-making. Even teams working in a hierarchy should discuss the leadership question. In such circumstances, the process often works better if the current boss relinquishes their role for the purpose of the experiment.

B. ASSIGNING ROLES AND RESPONSIBILITIES

One of the most effective ways of making meetings more purposeful and managing the whole experiment process is to assign roles and responsibilities to individuals or sub-groups in the team. Typically, these can include:

Change and people management   Here the focus needs to be on the four groups of stakeholders that we highlighted earlier in this section. The main responsibility is to ensure that people are engaged and informed at the appropriate level. This would include maintaining the stakeholder map and communication plan and monitoring internal and external relationships.

Learning   Experimentation is about learning and building upon that learning. Even if a hypothesis is unproven, the experiment remains a success if information is gained that influences the ensuing decisions. We recommend that teams nominate an individual who captures the learning from all perspectives as the experiment progresses. Too often we find that after a lengthy and complex experiment, many of the earlier lessons are lost.

Rigour and results   This role is about monitoring progress from the initial stages of the experiment through to the results so as to ensure that the appropriate degree of rigour is being applied. The template described earlier and the downloadable guide will be important tools in this process. Some of the questions that this sub-group would need to review and discuss with the wider team include:

- Do our original assumptions still hold true?
- Are we making new assumptions as the experiment develops?
- Do we have the appropriate baseline measures already in place?

- What is the early/interim feedback telling us?:
  - Are we getting the information we need?
  - Do we need to change anything about the interventions?
  - Are our measures still appropriate?
  - Do we need additional measures to test the hypothesis?
  - Is there evidence of Hawthorne or John Henry effects? (See Appendix A.)
  - Have any unexpected extraneous variables emerged?
  - Are we confident there is no cross-contamination between the experiment and control groups?

DOWNLOAD at www.koganpage.com/BusExp

Guide – OR10. Monitoring and review

Q5. What do the most successful teams do?

Earlier chapters provided examples of experiments addressing a variety of topics using the single six-step process. We would not have selected them if they were not good examples, but we are often asked: 'how can we avoid the pitfalls and what really makes a good experiment?' In the hundreds of experiments in which we have been involved, the following 12 characteristics are those we most commonly observe among successful teams.

1. CREATE THE RIGHT ENVIRONMENT

The best teams create a collective mindset that embraces curiosity. They are prepared to be bold, to take risks and accept that 'failure' may be an option. The best teams are prepared to challenge organizational norms and current ways of doing things. They have a 'democratized' approach that encourages an open dialogue and provides general direction but is not bound by hierarchies and top–down directives. They are aware of their individual and collective strengths and weaknesses and assign roles and responsibilities accordingly.

2. TAKE TIME TO CHOOSE THE TOPIC

If the topic is not already clearly evident, the best teams take time to generate and discuss topic ideas. They invest time and energy in ensuring that the selected option meets a set of criteria – that it adds value to the business, that it is 'doable' and that it energizes them. They rarely close down too early and continue to be open to new ideas even when shortlisting others.

3. TAKE TIME TO UNDERSTAND THE PROBLEM OR OPPORTUNITY

After selecting a topic, or even at the shortlist stage, the best teams take time to really understand the issue. They spend time talking with others to get different perspectives and learn from them. They get underneath the issue and do not allow the investigative process to rush them into a premature solution.

4. INVOLVE AND LEARN FROM OTHERS

This is not about those immediately involved in the experiment but a wider spectrum of contributors. The best teams look beyond the immediate challenge and learn by widening their horizons. Internally, it can include senior sponsors, specialists or other functions and countries in the business. Externally, it can include competitors, other industries, professional bodies and academia.

5. CREATE OPTIONS

The best teams expand the portfolio of choices, whether of topic options or experimental interventions that can test the hypothesis. Experimentation has a rhythm of creating choices and then making choices.

6. WORK THE HYPOTHESIS

Too many teams think that simply defining a clear hypothesis is sufficient. They believe that as long as it challenges assumptions and states the measurable outcomes, that is sufficient. The best teams certainly do that, but they *also live* with the hypothesis throughout the process. They continue to interrogate and challenge themselves about every word of the hypothesis, using it as a monitoring device throughout the experiment progression.

7. MANAGE THE ORGANIZATION

Those experimenting in organizations must manage the system. The best teams are mindful that senior-level sponsorship is important to support and challenge them in equal measure. During the process, it can be helpful in procuring funding, accessing resources or involving other departments. On completion of the experiment, organizational buy-in may be required to apply the recommendations.

8. EMBRACE THE SCIENCE

The best teams impose the appropriate level of rigour to ensure the validity of the experiment and the reliability of data. They take time to consider the 'scientific' requirements such as representation, sample size, culture, control/experiment group comparators, baseline metrics and external influences.

9. PLAN FOR A 'PROJECT' BUT RETAIN AN EXPERIMENTAL MINDSET

The best teams recognize the differences between an experiment and a project and how and where project management skills should be applied. Experiments are not projects per se, but they *do* require project management skills. The best teams develop a robust project plan that includes roles, responsibilities, realistic timelines, monitoring reviews, stakeholder mapping and communication plans.

10. PLAN FOR CHANGE

Experiments invariably test a proposal to *change* something – that is their nature. Within the organization, therefore, there will be winners and losers. It is important to recognize this. Some people may feel threatened by the outcome of the experiment. The best teams recognize that intellectual and emotional needs deserve careful consideration. Planning for change also reinforces the need for a strong narrative to share with stakeholders.

11. MONITOR AND ADAPT

As the experiment gets under way, the best teams start drawing information at early stages to determine whether the intervention is providing the right data to test the hypothesis. They are ready to adapt or even start again if the experiment is not performing as planned.

12. ANALYSE AND QUESTION

When gathering the data and coming to conclusions, the best teams adopt a sceptical mindset. They avoid the temptation of confirmation bias – fitting their results to prove the hypothesis. The best teams begin by questioning any influences on the data and its statistical significance. From the outset, they look for possible flaws in the experimental design and avoid premature conclusions in interpreting the data. Through this impartial process, they come to a surer set of findings and recommendations.

Evaluate

Analyse and interpret the results. Recommend actions and next steps

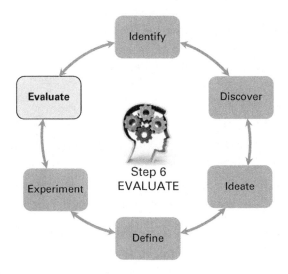

Throughout the experiment, the teams should be monitoring the validity and reliability of the data as they emerge, rather than waiting for *all* the results. In some cases, this may require adjustments in the experimental design if the interim results are not providing information that is statistically significant. In other cases, it may mean reviewing the measures themselves and determining whether there are alternative ways of calibrating the outcome. This is often frustrating but illustrates the uncertainty of experimentation.

Proof of hypothesis

A **proven hypothesis** leads to the implications for action. There may be sufficient confidence in the data to implement the findings straight away. On other occasions a more phased approach is required. This may be as part of a planned follow-on experiment to gain further evidence or as a staged rollout to manage risks.

> We described earlier a staged rollout with the HR consultancy in the Netherlands that experimented with new ways of introducing new technology. The experiment was conducted in Belgium and the Netherlands and, with a proven hypothesis, was then rolled out across Europe. The additional information gained allowed the team to refine their approach further and it was then tested and implemented globally. In this way a series of assumptions are tested, and even more information was gathered to enable the risks and complexity to be managed.

However, a proven hypothesis does not necessarily mean that the results can be immediately implemented or moved to a second phase. Very often the results of an experiment prompt more questions than answers. The hypothesis may be proven but the information gained can also reveal unexpected findings or spark new ideas.

An **unproven hypothesis** can mean that the resulting data from the test was insufficient to conclude that the hypothesis was proven or disproven. There can be a variety of reasons for that outcome, but it may mean that the testing process itself was flawed. In other words, it was not sufficiently rigorous to provide confidence in the results and there was little of value to be learned. This is where the word 'failure' can sometimes be used.

A **disproven hypothesis** is where sufficient evidence was gained to make a decision but that the hypothesis was incorrect. Something that the team speculated as being true has been found to be false. This in itself is a discovery. A disproven hypothesis, therefore, should not be seen as 'failure'. Even if the experiment did not produce the anticipated outcomes, it will have provided an opportunity to learn and may have pre-empted a mistaken decision. It may also encourage the team to re-test a slightly modified hypothesis.

Confidence in the recommendations

Even after the data has been analysed at the end of the experiment, there are occasions when teams still seek greater certainty before claiming whether the hypothesis is proven or disproven. In earlier chapters we described how the experiment process means living with ambiguity and uncertainty. Decisions are made with an element of doubt and risk that may be alien to 'normal' business practice. The same discomfort can be experienced at the EVALUATE stage, where the final results may not provide complete answers or where doubts remain about proposals for next steps.

Promoting a scientific approach certainly enhances the rationality of decision-making in business but can never provide 100 per cent surety. Even the best clinical trials fail to achieve that. However, the experiment should allow decisions and proposals to be made with a 'reasonable degree of confidence'. Inevitably, the interpretation of 'reasonable degree of confidence' will vary among those involved and it is for that reason we provide a framework to assist teams.

Whether the experiment team is part of a large organization presenting findings to an executive board or a small business owner communicating results to employees, there are ways in which teams can be 'reasonably confident' if they are **CLEAR** about the following:

Conduct of the experiment. The experiment has been conducted with the appropriate level of scientific rigour. There is confidence that the process will stand up to challenge.

Limitations. The scope of the experiment is clear. For example, further experiments may be needed to test the hypothesis in other areas of the business and across a wider population.

Expected results. Experimentation means keeping an open mind when interpreting results to avoid confirmation bias. However, when considering whether a hypothesis is proven or disproven, it can be useful (with a degree of caution) to consider how different the results would have to have been to change the verdict.

Assumptions. As with limitations above, any proposal for next steps needs to revisit the original assumptions underpinning the experiment and speculate on what new assumptions might be made in any further experimentation.

Reliability. In addition to the experiment being conducted in a robust way, the results themselves need to be statistically significant. Proof of reliability will increase confidence that the results did not happen by chance. (Appendix A provides greater detail of experimental terminology.)

BEING CLEAR (EVALUATE IN ACTION)

The news that a vaccine had been found to counter the Covid-19 virus with a 90 per cent success rate was greeted with relief and excitement in late 2020. The scientists at Pfizer/BioNTech were cautiously optimistic but, as clinicians, were keen to reinforce that there were still many questions to be answered. However, they were 'reasonably confident' of the results and sufficiently so to share the outcomes of the experiment to the world's media and regulatory bodies. As they explained the next steps, they expressed the spirit of the CLEAR philosophy.

CONDUCT. They were confident that the testing process and sample sizes involving 44,000 people in three continents with age ranges of 8–80 were robust. They felt assured that the relatively straightforward A/B tests had been conducted with the right level of scientific rigour.

LIMITATIONS. The scientists explained that there were caveats. More data was required, there was still no proof it would prevent transmission, the length of immunity was uncertain and there were still some doubts about effectiveness with elderly patients. There were also concerns about storage temperatures and transport.

EXPECTED RESULTS. Expectations of results for medical trials will vary. A flu vaccine is estimated to be 67 per cent effective on average, and when scientists began the Covid-19 research, they deemed 50 per cent effectiveness to be acceptable. The result that it was 90 per cent effective after the first few trials exceeded all expectations.

ASSUMPTIONS. The assumptions involved in the early stages of the research were numerous. Not least was the assumption that the use of a new genetic code (mRNA) approach could replace conventional vaccines. Rolling out the vaccine involved a new set of assumptions; for example, that deep cold storage and distribution facilities would be available where needed.

RELIABILITY. The 44,000 sample, ranging from Brazilian beach goers to Berlin office workers, was split evenly between those inoculated against the virus and others with a placebo jab. It took time before a 'suitable' number of participants had caught the disease. 94 people showed symptoms of the disease with only 8 in the vaccine group. The statistical significance of this was reinforced a week later when ongoing trials showed that, out of 170 people with the disease, only 8 were from the vaccine group, resulting in a 95 per cent effectiveness.

The message for business experiment teams in the EVALUATE stage is CLEAR. By demonstrating a robust process, by explaining the scope and limitations of the experiment and by using reliable results, recommendations and next steps can be proposed with 'reasonable confidence'. A downloadable guide is provided to support you in structuring your recommendations.

DOWNLOAD at www.koganpage.com/BusExp

Guide – OR11. Structuring the recommendations

Summary

Our intention in this chapter has been to take the reader through a process for experimentation and to provide practical tools and techniques on the way. A small senior management team in a large organization has been the exemplar, but it is emphasized that the same process can be used for individual entrepreneurs and small businesses. The process is not meant to be set in stone. It can, and should, be adapted to suit different situations, for example, when there is less rigour required or time constraints apply. But the aim has been to provide you with a process that can stand on its own for even the most complex business experiments. We have used it with experiment teams on many occasions and can testify to its efficacy.

And yet... despite the many benefits and its contribution to business decision-making, experimentation is rarely the first tool to be grasped in the managerial toolbox. There are some organizations that have been able to embrace it with vigour and others that struggle to wrestle themselves away from traditional management practices. In the next chapters we look at how organizations can develop an experimental culture and how the individual intrapreneur can play their part.

Note

1 Simon, H A (1996) *The Sciences of the Artificial*, MIT Press, Boston

09

Accelerating the change:
The experimentalist

We described earlier how Stefan, our medical client based in China, felt both frustrated and unsettled when faced with the experience of experimentation. He felt his usual, orderly and structured approach to his work had been turned upside down as he grappled with the uncertainty of this new way of thinking. He found that the behaviours and skills that had served him so well in the past had only limited effect in this new environment. At that time, our way of supporting clients like Stefan was to explain the differences between 'normal' management practices and what experimentation entailed. While we may have succeeded in managing their expectations, we realized that it was not the complete answer and we had to do more.

In such cases, we could see that individuals *knew* what to expect and knew, to a large extent, what needed to be done. They were aware of the behavioural changes required and could see how experimentation might be integrated with other management tools. However, they were encountering obstacles and finding it difficult to put into practice. Our role was to help make the process easier. In this chapter we describe two ways in which we tried to do so:

1 **First,** we wanted experimentation to become an established process and as interchangeable in its use as the more established management practices. Our aim was to show managers *how* they can loosen the grip of traditional methods and provide them with

another way of working. We wanted to show them *how* they can disrupt the cycle and *choose* to become an experimental manager through a **systems thinking approach**.

2 **Second,** we had to find ways to accelerate the behavioural transition and ensure that the changes became permanent rather than transitory. We wanted to make attributes like enquiry, curiosity and challenge as natural to managers as scheduling and cost management. Our aim was for managers to be able to swap intuitively from one skill or behaviour to another. It was for these reasons that we introduced the concept of the **personal experiment**.

We have already remarked upon the fact that knowing what needs to be done does not necessarily lead to its being done, however compelling the argument. We explore this paradox further by looking more closely at the psychological causes of the knowing–doing gap.

The knowing–doing gap

You may find in your own organization that, while much of the **talk** is about innovation and transformation, most of the **action** is concerned with short-term performance targets. The **rhetoric** of management may well be visionary, but the **reality** of life back in the office, under the pressure to perform, is very different. As an experimentalist, putting bold ideas into practice is a rare skill. Changing what we **do** feels much harder than changing what we **know**.

Jeffrey Pfeffer and Robert Sutton, both of them professors at Stanford Graduate School of Business, have called this 'the knowing–doing gap'.[1] They suggest that companies invariably know what needs to be done, and yet abstain from actually doing it. The same applies to the individual. Managers are aware that they should be taking certain actions or behaving in a particular way but find it difficult to do so.

Even in our personal lives we see it regularly. People know they should be taking more exercise, eating more healthily or stopping smoking, yet seem unable to make such a lasting lifestyle change. The same might be said of the list of dos and don'ts that we produced for the experimentalist in Chapter 6. The individual knows that they all make sense, but they can appear a daunting, even overwhelming, task – and lasting change is thereby deferred.

The organizational environment will have a large influence on this inertia but there are also some individual characteristics that make it even harder to close the knowing–doing gap:

- fear of failure and reluctance to take the risk;
- resistance to any departure from entrenched behaviours that have brought past success;
- difficulty in breaking away from established management practices;
- an unwillingness to challenge a deep belief system;
- unease with provocation;
- disinclination to be seen as a disruptor.

In this chapter, we argue that experimentation is a technique for closing the knowing–doing gap at both an individual level and as a way of influencing the organizational culture. For many, this will be a brave step, but there are two ways of doing it.

1. Systems thinking:
Choosing to be an experimental manager

With the passage of time, both personal beliefs and corporate assumptions can meld into one and harden into dogma; learned behaviours, which may well have served their original purpose well, become obdurate habits; and the inclination to challenge the resulting status quo becomes a taboo.

In Figure 9.1 we depict the essence of the problem, and how experimentation can be the remedy.

This system of thinking builds on a concept we introduced earlier in the book. In place of the twin poles of control and learning we now have dogmatic thinking (fixed mindset) on the left, and critical

FIGURE 9.1   Where we get stuck, and how to get unstuck

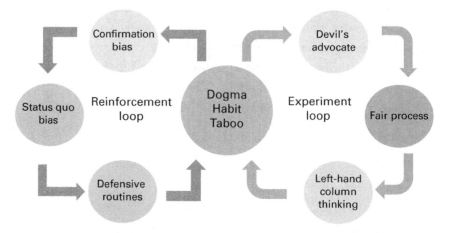

thinking (growth mindset) on the right. At the centre there are the rigid beliefs, ingrained habits and shared taboos that define our mindset and hold us captive. However strongly we may wish to break free, three particular pathologies, shown in the left-hand loop, reinforce the existing state of affairs. The countervailing loop on the right represents the experimental mindset, consisting of various techniques of thinking that can loosen the chains of stasis. The gist of the argument conveyed in Figure 9.1 is that most organizations would benefit from a rebalancing of priorities away from the reinforcement mentality and towards a more experimental approach.

The reinforcement loop

Three factors among many explain how the components of the left-hand loop contribute towards inertia.

The **confirmation bias** is our inclination to take notice only of data that is congruent with our prior set of beliefs and values. We screen out and ignore data that could weaken or challenge our convictions. We subconsciously censor what we do not wish to hear. Conversely, we privilege information that corroborates our view of things.

The **status quo bias** is our emotional preference for the way things happen to be. We are suspicious of change, if only because most changes in the past have only made things worse and wrought disappointment. It is akin to our trust in traditional customs, conventions and routines. If they hadn't served us well in the past (we say to ourselves), they would have been replaced long ago.

Defensive routines emanate from the unspoken contract we all have within the firm not to challenge certain prevailing assumptions, practices and principles. In most organizations, their members will know what is undiscussable. Furthermore, they will know that this issue itself is undiscussable.

Together these three habits of thought fiercely protect the prevailing state of affairs and disable attempts to interrogate it or tamper with it.

The experimental loop

Turning to the experimental loop, these are three techniques for loosening the grip that the status quo has on us.

Playing devil's advocate is one way of countering the confirmation bias. We decide to pay attention to opposing arguments. We encourage disagreement and debate. We expand our network to include those of different opinions and persuasions. We read newspapers whose political stance differs from our own. We take particular notice of anything that takes us by surprise, on the assumption that this constitutes a challenge to our natural way of thinking. We respect those who speak up in meetings and challenge anything that looks like settling into a premature consensus.

Fair process is closely related to this form of open dialogue. Recognizing that, in any organization, no one can expect to win every argument and that therefore there is always the danger of losing the loyalty of those on the 'losing' side, the idea is that ways must be found to earn their wholehearted commitment to the implementation of the policy. Fair process, a form of procedural justice, is the method by which we win their support even though they were on the losing side of the argument. To this end, they must feel that their ideas and arguments were at least heard and respected and built upon before being rejected rationally in favour of other ideas. Only then will they feel able to fully support the implementation of policies with which they don't entirely agree. **Mutual understanding** is a version of fair process. It is the idea that, in a meeting, you are only allowed to air your disagreement with someone if, first, you spell out their argument, and second, they agree that you have expressed it at least as well as they did themselves. This process of active listening and mutual respect builds a culture that is much more comfortable challenging the status quo.

Left-hand column thinking is a technique invented by Chris Argyris, a Harvard Business School professor, for tackling defensive behaviour, particularly when we are insufficiently open and candid in conversations with our colleagues at work.[2] We hide our thoughts and feelings without necessarily being aware that we are doing so. Things that may need to be said and shared go unsaid and unshared. In a meeting, for example, a thought crosses our mind but, judging it to be contentious, we self-censor it. In doing so, we disrespect our colleagues by not trusting them with our innermost thoughts. The quality of the conversation deteriorates as people refrain from saying what is on their mind, out of fear of being controversial or critical. As a result, only what is banal gets shared. Left-hand column thinking comprises six steps:

1 Choose a significant, but difficult, conversation or meeting from the recent past.

2 Take a piece of paper and divide it into two vertical columns.

3 In the right-hand column, record the conversation as faithfully as you can ('I said this, then he said that, then I said…').

4 In the left-hand column, record what you were thinking and feeling as each of these things were being said.

5 Comparing both columns, what was different between what you were saying and what you were thinking and feeling?

6 Ask yourself how more of your internal thoughts and feelings might have found greater expression and lent the conversation or meeting greater integrity.

Using active listening (fair process) techniques, playing devil's advocate or using a process like left-hand column thinking are three ways to break the cycle that reinforces established behaviours and identify the things that need to change. Ultimately, these ways of thinking and the changes we make will only be impactful if individuals are brave enough to challenge convention, and that is why we encourage personal experimentation.

2. The personal experiment

Even with motivated managers, things can become complicated when they try to practise new behaviours or different ways of doing things. As experimentalists, they may need to be democratic and inclusive at one moment, but at the next moment, in the context of the 'day job', may have to assert greater control or provide stronger direction. Alternating between styles can feel disjointed, confusing and even inauthentic to others.

Thus, reticence to try out something new is understandable. It is why we encourage the individual to conduct a personal experiment. By focusing on just one or two competences, the risks and scope of the experiment can be managed and shared with others. In this way, experimentation provides a licence to act in different and varied ways. The personal experiment can follow the same six-step model as in Chapter 8, acting as a 'taster' for the methodology when later applied to a business topic for the main experiment.

How do you measure up?

As with an organizational experiment, the personal experiment begins by identifying a problem. In this case the 'problem' relates to the experimental competences that need to be improved.

Most managers and executives will have received formal and informal feedback about their strengths and weaknesses through performance management discussions, leadership assessment surveys and 360 feedback processes. However, it is rare that they are able to explore more deeply the 'experimental competences', such as their attitudes to risk, their natural curiosity, their willingness to be challenged or their desire for perfection.

This is why we have referred back to the list of dos and don'ts in Chapter 6. It is an ideal starting point for the personal experiment. It is not meant to be a checklist to be ticked off on your journey to becoming an 'ideal' experimentalist. However, it does provide the basis of a self-assessment questionnaire, encouraging individuals to 'hold up a mirror' and assess their strengths and opportunities for improvement.

DOWNLOAD at www.koganpage.com/BusExp

Guide – OR13. Personal assessment questionnaire

Using the six-step process

Table 9.1 shows how your personal experiment can follow the same methodology as that described in the last chapter.

TABLE 9.1   Steps to take in your personal experiment

IDENTIFY	What is the focus of your personal experiment? What needs to change to make you a better leader? Use the personal assessment questionnaire, as well as 360 feedback and coaching discussions, to identify two or three skills that you need to improve.
DISCOVER	Explore these skills by considering what impact each of them has had or is having on your leadership capability. Get the views of your boss, your peers and your team members to discover their perspectives and how your attitudes and behaviour affect them.
IDEATE	What options and opportunities do you have to address the identified issues? What are the things you might need to do differently in each case? What have you never tried – but should try – to address the issue? What have others done in similar situations? What other sources for potential solutions can you explore?
DEFINE	Now select **one** of these options that has the potential to make a significant impact if addressed. If this particular skill were to improve, what could be the impact? What will people be saying? How will you feel? What business benefit might there be? Formulate your chosen resolution as a hypothesis in the following format: 'If I do X, then Y will be the result.'
EXPERIMENT	How will you test your hypothesis? Where/when/how will you conduct the experiment? How will you involve others? How long will the experiment run? How will you measure the result? Who else can help you interpret the experiment outcomes?
EVALUATE	What conclusions have you drawn from the experiment? Is the information sufficient to make decisions about next steps? What do you need to keep doing or start doing differently? Who do you need to inform? How will you sustain the changes? Which of the other skills identified in steps 1–3 might you consider for the next experiment?

Summary

Experimentation is as much about attitudes and mindsets as it is about applying a methodology. In many cases, it requires individuals to adjust behaviours that may have served them well in the past. We described in this chapter how that is never an easy task, especially for those in organizations that remain firmly wedded to traditional management practices. It is why we have described a two-way approach to help overcome the obstacles and accelerate the changes.

First, we introduced a systems thinking approach and demonstrated ways in which an organization can reduce its reliance on control and planning. Our proposal here is that, by breaking the cycle, a better balance can be created between the control and experiment loops. Evidence of this organizational shift then provides a clear message to others that curiosity is encouraged and that organizational norms can be challenged.

The second part of this chapter focused on the way in which the individual can 'experiment with experimentation'. We proposed a way of using the same six-step methodology as a personal experiment. In this way, the individual becomes familiar with the process – using it in a contained way that still provides value.

Notes

1 Pfeffer, J and Sutton, R I (2000) *The Knowing–Doing Gap: How smart companies turn knowledge into action*, Harvard Business School Press, Boston
2 Argyris, C (1994) *Overcoming Organizational Defences*, Prentice Hall, Hoboken, NJ

10

What characterizes an experimental organization?

Business experimentation, if it is to be more than the latest fad or a top–down initiative, needs to be more than a toolkit. It will only deliver if it is embedded in a culture that embraces learning through trial and error. So, what are the minimal requirements for claiming to be an experimental culture? How would an outsider recognize it? What are the signature traits? And what sets it apart from a non-experimental organization?

First, there will be a deep-seated understanding that running a business is a long-term learning race, in which profit is essentially a return on the truth of the assumptions underpinning the strategy of the firm, relative to that of rivals. Thus, business is, above all, a creative and disruptive activity. It is imbued with the notion of progress. More than any other class of activity, it has shaped the modern world, and the ways in which we live and work. Nicolas Rashevsky, who looked at history through the eyes of a mathematician, has argued that trade, since its origins, has been the great catalyst of civilization.[1] Historically, the exchange of goods brought different peoples and cultures together. The great markets of the ancient world, such as Palmyra, the Silk Road and Venice, acted as crossing-points for inter-cultural exchange. Trade fomented curiosity. The mixing of ideas inspired fresh perspectives. If business is to continue to be a dynamic and civilizing force, it needs to retain – and strengthen – its zest for creativity and innovation. Experimentation, the art of asking bewitching questions and testing imaginative answers, lies at the heart of this skill.

Second, there will be the skill of designing and conducting experiments that give clear and reliable answers to well-formed questions. This is a competence that comes with practice. To some extent, it can be taught. But a culture of experimentation is deeper than the possession of strong intention, right belief and honed skill.

Dimensions of a corporate culture

A famous metaphor of what is meant by culture is Edward Hall's image of the iceberg. Some parts are above the waterline and visible; other parts are below it and hidden. The visible parts are what Hall called the conscious, explicitly learned culture, such as objective knowledge and purposive actions. The invisible part, the implicitly learned, unconscious culture, which Hall believed to be the larger and more influential part, includes tacit knowledge, subliminal assumptions, embedded values and automatic thought patterns.

At a national level, the visible culture includes such things as language, food and dress; whereas the hidden culture includes concepts of justice, attitudes to authority and rules of conduct. Within a company, what is visible is the organization chart, the strategic plan and the job description; while what is less visible, and much more difficult to codify, are the rules of success, the freedom of action and the hierarchy of values. The former is relatively easy to change, if only because it is conscious and codified; the latter, being more mysterious, is harder to articulate, let alone change.

Culture is how we behave when we're not thinking or paying attention. It is those things we take for granted, the assumptions that we take as read, the behaviours that have become non-reflexive habits and the values that have become second nature to us. They are all there because they once served a purpose. They made sense. They felt right. But long after their raison d'être has become redundant, they remain a part of us, still shaping our behaviour. What determines corporate performance – for good or ill – is mainly the stuff that is **not** articulated, and **not** acknowledged. It is as though a ghost in the machine is directing affairs.

An experimental culture is one that makes a concerted attempt to surface and codify this substrate of beliefs, habits and priorities, if only to test its continuing validity. We pay particular attention to those decisions we make that feel too automatic. We notice those habits that seem to serve no obvious purpose. By doing this archaeology on our own mental models, we place ourselves in a stronger position to conduct life-changing experiments. The best experiments tend to be those that test the things that have always been around but with no obvious rationale.

So, let us return to the questions with which we began. How would you recognize an experimental culture and what sets an experimental organization apart from others? What should an experimental organization aspire to be?

10 features of the experimental organization

In our work with a range of businesses across many industry sectors, we have rarely found an organization that displays *all* of the characteristics we describe below. However, they are listed here to represent the most influential features we observe in experimental organizations. At the end of this chapter there will be an opportunity for you to benchmark your own organization against the characteristics we feature here.

1. There is an implicit rulebook

In experimental cultures people know what it stands for, and what it entails. The economic case for experimentation is well understood. It is seen neither as a fad, nor a panacea for whatever is ailing the organization. It is regarded simply as a disciplined method of acting rationally and it is understood that there is a right (and wrong) way of doing it. Managers take responsibility for equipping themselves with this skill. There will be publicized examples of effective experiments. The distinction between an experiment and a project, and between a good and a bad experiment, is clear. There are rules of the game. They may be minimal, but they matter. What is the implicit contract? For example, who has the right to conduct how many experiments at what cost over what period of time? How will success be defined? We suggest that a model experiment is one that is inspired by a question that, if answered well and applied with skill, yields a competitive advantage to the firm. If experimentation is well defined, and everyone understands it, it's then much easier to notice whether or not it is contributing to the performance of the firm. There is a recognition that 'this is the way we do things round here'.

2. Bureaucracy is untangled

In experimental organizations, no one is waiting to be given a motive, reason or excuse to initiate change. There is a tacit understanding that the raison d'être of being in business in a competitive marketplace is to be continuously questioning the status quo and, by doing so, creating wealth from original insights and pathbreaking practices. Change is not something that happens to the firm; it is a path that is actively chosen by the firm.

In an experimental organization, shaping the future is seen to be better achieved by trial and error than by planning and implementation. Much greater attention is paid to experimentation and discovery than to cost-cutting and operational efficiency. A greater share of capital is invested in these activities. People naturally sign up to this adventure. Their creativity finds its voice. They feel heard.

Experimentation is rare in cultures that rely upon compliance or fear. We should be able to bring into the workplace the same fearless inventiveness that is natural and effortless when we are at home, or with friends, or on holiday. It is important not to drain the firm of its entrepreneurial vitality by only operating within the parameters of predictability, controllability and measurability. Challenging the firm's orthodoxies is not seen as an act of disloyalty or disrespect but an expression of allegiance and enthusiasm. Like everything of significance in an enterprise, they are acts of bravery and generosity; they are gifts from individuals to the collective.

3. 'Best practice' is questioned

The experimental firm sets its sights on going beyond the piecemeal engineering initiatives that, in earlier times, went by such names as skunk works, innovation labs, brainstorming sessions, knowledge management, daily scrums and hackathons. Effective as some of them have certainly been, they have not challenged the sacred cows of bureaucracy. Our organizational models have changed less in 100 years than almost any other technology and, for the most part, these types of interventions have left the organizational model and its associated management practices unscathed. They may even have protected them.

In an experimental organization we see the practices that hold back organizational learning being strongly challenged. Very little of any consequence is achieved by dutiful obedience to 'best practice'. Progress is made mainly by those who choose to see a world of possibilities and, despite the risks of personal embarrassment or even opprobrium, take ownership of the experimentation necessary to bring it to fruition. Work is regarded not as a penance but a privilege.

4. Latent talent is liberated

In an experimental culture, a greater proportion of the optimistic and creative talent available to the organization finds expression. Indeed, this is a fundamental criterion – and metric – of 'efficiency' in an experimental organization. What is its capacity to tap into the energy and goodwill of its members, and how much effort goes into increasing this proportion? The idea is to make the collective at least as creative, resourceful and courageous as the individuals who belong to it. This runs counter to the tacit rules that regulate less experimental organizations, namely: the top knows best, keep your head down, don't rock the boat, look busy, toe the line, be careful and wait patiently for promotion. Perhaps we exaggerate, but even so, such a culture – or the whiff of such a culture – is unlikely to attract the renegades, creatives and subversives upon which an experimental culture relies. Those who take their models of success entirely from the past are unlikely to be the inventors of the future.

5. Gatekeepers are bypassed

When power is vested mainly in a few people at the top, they inevitably become the arbiters of which ideas are to be taken seriously. As the gatekeepers of the culture, the pace of change can be no more radical than what they personally find acceptable and comfortable. The fate of the organization rests disproportionately in the hands of a rather small coterie of senior executives, whose own success relied more on competence and compliance than creativity and courage. Experimental cultures are acutely aware of the fate of totalitarian societies and take these lessons to heart in the leadership behaviours they espouse. They are aware of the contradiction between a top-heavy organization and one steeped in the experimental ethic. The challenge of modern business is to find the right balance between control and freedom of expression, and between alignment and diversity of thought. In each case, both sides of the equation have their value. However, an experimental culture is constantly alert to the dangers of a natural reversion to the bureaucratic norms.

6. Curiosity is aroused

Experimental organizations stimulate creativity more by questions than by plans or processes. Three particular sets of questions help focus attention upon topics that matter:

PERSISTENT DERAILMENT

What are the dilemmas that never seem to get resolved? Which are the tradeoffs that we keep getting wrong? For example, how do we square short-term pressures with longer-term interests? How do we weigh the interests of different groups of stakeholders? What is the right mix of rationality and playfulness? Experimental organizations seek to discover the sweet spot in each of these dilemmas.

SHARED INCOMPETENCE

What *can't* we do? What do we and our competitors consistently get wrong? Where is the core incompetence of our industry? In every sector, there will be problems that every firm finds infuriatingly diffi-cult. This lacuna may relate to incompetence in the market for talent, for customers or for capital. It may have to do with design, service or reputation. It may take the form of obstacles, inhibitions or fears, whether real or imaginary.

IMMINENT DISRUPTION

What aspect of the future gives us greatest cause for concern? To what future state of affairs do we *not* have a solution? Like a rabbit in the headlights, we feel frozen. We frame disruption as a threat to our own business rather than an opportunity to threaten others. The dreaded acronym, VUCA (volatility, uncertainty, complexity, ambigu-ity), is treated as something that the world is inflicting on business rather than something that business, by nature of its intrinsic dyna-mism, is contributing to the world. Passivity runs deep. Many firms persist in casting themselves as victims, not inventors of the future. The future has not been written. Experimentation can shape it.

7. Fallibility is accepted

The most basic fact about an experiment is that it is unpredictable. It has one of two answers to any hypothesis: corroborated and there-fore assumed true, or refuted and therefore assumed false. Only *after* the experiment has been conducted do we know which answer it gives to the question. This can produce frustration and anxiety in the mind of the bureaucrat, whose natural hostility towards the unexpected means that they prefer to deal with ready-made solutions rather than open problems.

The acknowledgement of human fallibility and the importance of open-mindedness are intrinsic to a belief in the necessity of experimentation, and the central role it needs to play in business. For every Amazon Prime or Kindle, there are 10 or 20 equivalents of Amazon Destinations, or the Amazon Fire mobile phone, just two of their well-publicized 'failures'.

Experimentation goes hand in hand with disappointment and impatience. The experimental journey, if it is to be bold and productive, will often be a case of two steps forward and one step back. There is no such thing as a smooth, predictable, risk-free experimental path. The important point here is that a genuine experimentation culture will provide the support, encouragement and trust sufficient to compensate for these moments of tribulation.

8. Connectivity is pursued

Why do the smokers in a company come up with more creative ideas than their non-smoking colleagues?[2] Because they stand outside in ad hoc gatherings talking about whatever is on their mind. This may be apocryphal, but it contains an important truth. Conversations, particularly among diverse talents and across organizational boundaries, are more likely to yield imaginative thoughts and ideas than formalized meetings with set goals, formal agendas and time constraints, particularly among well-established, overly familiar teams.

Listening in on each other's stories, learning from their adventures, championing their achievements and spreading the learning are grist to the experimental mill. Inspired by Google's famous '20 per cent time' policy, which has always sought to encourage personal creativity and collective innovation, Web Profits, a SaaS marketing agency, schedules company-wide monthly meetings for ideas and findings to be shared, with cash prizes for those who discover the important breakthroughs (with half of the winnings paid up front and the balance paid as soon as the idea has been profitably implemented). Connectivity is an important contributor to an experimental culture.

9. Outcomes are measured

Measuring the performance of experimentation in the organization sends a clear message that it is a vital component of the business. Everyone is led to appreciate that it is not only important, but also that they themselves are expected to be key players in the creation and sustenance of this culture. Measures are regularly taken of several indices: the number of experiments conducted; the cost, scale and longevity of each experiment; the proportion of them that come to a conclusion that changes minds, influences policy and affects behaviour; and, of these, the proportion that produce a positive return on investment. A dedication to accurate measurement is itself a catalyst of ever more successful experimentation.

10. Learning is embodied

The accumulation of hard-won knowledge from experimentation is documented and shared. The best organizations do this in both formal and informal ways, using knowledge-sharing platforms or simple word of mouth. This habit replicates, of course, the method of science and the importance of keeping tabs on the development of knowledge, from whatever source. Putting experimentation at the heart of the business has the effect of nurturing the growth mindset. People share their thoughts, talk about ideas and learn from each other's experiments and insights. It is a recurring theme in meetings and emails. It comes up naturally whenever there is an important decision to be made, or there is a sticking point, or there is a challenge to which there is no easy answer. When this becomes an organizational habit, it has the effect of building momentum towards an inquisitive and innovative culture.

Experimentation is thought to **matter**.

Summary

We began with a chapter heading that asked the question: 'What characterizes an experimental organization?' We have described 10 features that, from our experience, answer the question. Collectively, they may be described as a 'habit' where experimentation is **second nature** to everyone in the organization. It is a widespread proficiency where conducting a test needs neither permission nor prompting. It is not seen as a specialist skill but part and parcel of being a competent employee. Whenever there is a problem, a disagreement or an opportunity for innovation, it becomes the first call in seeking a potential remedy.

The downloadable guide allows you to assess your own organization alongside the 10 characteristics we describe. How well does *your* organization measure up?

Using your questionnaire responses as a starting point, the next two chapters describe tactics and techniques that will help you to develop an experimental culture in *your* business.

DOWNLOAD at www.koganpage.com/BusExp

Guide – OR12. Organizational assessment

Notes

1 Rashevsky, N (1968) *Looking at History Through Mathematics*, MIT Press, Boston

2 The evidence for this is slight, but read: Efficient While Lazy (25 January 2016) The hidden reason why smokers are often more creative than non smokers, efficientwhilelazy.com/the-hidden-reason-why-smokers-are-often-more-creative-than-non-smokers/ (archived at https://perma.cc/AM9N-XK3E)

11

Building an experimental culture

In the last chapter, we described what a fully fledged experimental organization would look and feel like, and how it would operate. We defined its distinctive cultural practices. Throughout the book, we have given reasons why such a culture, despite its appeal, is difficult to create and sustain.

In this chapter, we offer some methods by which these barriers can be overcome, and a genuinely experimental organization created. In doing so, we shall be challenging many of the assumptions that underpin most change management initiatives. In particular, we will argue that a culture of experimentation cannot be 'managed into being' or 'led from the top', if only because management and leadership are themselves two of the barriers.

We invite you to use this chapter to pause for a while and reflect on your own perceptions and experiences of culture change. Our aim is to inform, provoke and inspire in equal measure. We shall offer a different lens through which to view corporate renewal.

A thought experiment

Imagine if your company had no say in whom it employed. In common with its competitors, its workforce would be drawn at random from the same population, such that its human talent was indistinguishable from that of its rivals. How well would it perform? In other words, how much of its performance would be due to its system of management and how much to the skills of its people?

It is sometimes said that great companies are great because they have great people, and vice versa. In other words, the performance of a company is determined essentially by the talent that it can attract and retain. As a young business school professor, Jeffrey Pfeffer, now a leading organizational theorist, took this belief for granted, but when, later in life, he looked for evidence of this theory, he found that there was virtually none. What he did discover disturbed him because it was so unexpected. In a nutshell, he found that ordinary people in extraordinary organizations invariably outperform extraordinary people in ordinary organizations.[1]

The implications of this belief, if true, are dramatic: the performance of a company has much more to do with its organizational model (its systems, processes and policies) than its people (their capabilities, qualifications and character). Context counts more than raw talent. Thus, the art of management is to design a work environment that enables talent to flourish.

Naturally we will want to employ the most gifted people we can – but we should not rely on these gifts to determine overall performance.

Now, if it is true that it is the organizational model that sets the performance parameters – and for the purpose of this chapter, we shall assume that it is – we need to ask ourselves whether the standard management model serves companies well, or whether it fails them badly.

The first and most obvious point is that if the vast majority of firms use broadly the same management model, however sensible it may be, it cannot be the source of either corporate success or failure. Because it is shared by all, it has become a commodity and cannot therefore be a source of competitive advantage.

The second point to make is there are many intuitive reasons – and much empirical research – to suggest that the standard management model does *not* bring out the best in human beings.

The likelihood is that most firms are sharing the same suboptimal infrastructure. If true, this creates a huge opportunity for those firms who recognize this fact and set out to explore better ways of organizing work. This is where experimentation comes in. Our thesis is twofold: first, firms need to experiment with different ways of managing; and second, the way of managing that will be found to offer the greatest competitive advantage will be one based on experimentation.

A short history of managerialism

The bureaucratization and standardization of the ways in which people typically work together in organizations cramps creativity. The room for discretion, for trial and error, and for discovering new ways of working is exceptionally constrained. Individual employees simply don't have the licence to experiment with ideas that have the potential to radically enhance performance. Almost every learning and development programme today adopts as its agenda the themes of agility, digitalization, empowerment and engagement, but rarely is the managerial context in which these objectives are being sought up for debate, appraisal or reinvention.

What was the last idea that your colleagues shared with you that had the potential to raise the ceiling on innovation, to undo some of the harm that bureaucracy does, and to open up the discretionary space for innovation and experimentation?

The truth is that managerialism tends to **subtract** value from the talent at its disposal: the organization is **less** creative than those it employs. The whole is less than the sum of its parts. And the problem is getting **worse** with every year that passes. For example, the momentous changes wrought by outsourcing and offshoring – almost always driven by the search for global supply chains of ever lower costs – end up shrinking the opportunity for qualitative differentiation into an ever smaller segment of the value chain.

By definition, only one player in any industry can (temporally) win this game. The rest are losers, ceaselessly trying to catch up with the winner by sacrificing more and more quality to the sole cause and criterion of operational efficiency. This is a losing strategy that we have called 'the fatal bias' – and that Deloitte in particular has shown empirically to be a flawed business model.[2] Consultants and advisers often add to this commoditization by transferring 'best practice' from one client to another.

It is worth bringing to mind some of the organizational innovations of the last 100 years or more and reflecting upon their impact on the organizational model of managerialism. Invariably, they reinforced it rather than enhancing or subverting it: the invention of double-entry booking (and the foundations of financial accounting and budgeting); the concept of the division of labour; its application to the workplace in the form of the assembly line; Weber's theory of bureaucracy and the 'rationalization' of work practices; the invention of the joint stock company (and its cousin, the limited liability company); Edison's invention of the industrial research lab; Sloan's adoption of the divisional organizational structure; DuPont's invention of capital budgeting; Drucker's theory of management-by-objective and the core elements of strategic planning; Alderson's theory of the total marketing concept and its spinoff, brand management; the Toyota production system and processes of continuous improvement.

Pioneering though these innovations were, they did little to challenge the hierarchical and bureaucratic precepts of managerialism. In some cases, they strengthened them. What sets experimentation apart as an organizational principle is that it directly confronts both of these precepts. It is suspicious of expertise vested in authority and processes parading as 'best practice'. There is nothing in an experimental culture that is sacrosanct.

If experimentation is to be more than the latest management fad, it must be more ambitious. We have three benchmarks in mind:

- It must upset the status quo and challenge prevailing wisdom; in other words, it must feel risky and uncomfortable, particularly to those in authority.

- It must imply that many of the managerial structures and processes that we take for granted are flawed in some way, or counterproductive in today's environment.
- It must itself be an unfinished project; in other words, it is imperfect with plenty of potential, still to be explored and developed.

Business experimentation meets all three criteria: it is heretical, transformational and embryonic.

Three ways forward

How do you transform a corporate culture? How do you move from one set of processes, values and attitudes to another? What best induces individuals to alter their ways of working, thinking and acting? Change management is as old as the hills. Every issue of *Harvard Business Review* seems to have at least one article advocating a new method of changing an organization for the better. At the risk of oversimplification, these methods boil down to one of three distinctive techniques:

- **managing** the change, using bureaucracy;
- **leading** the change, using inspiration;
- **triggering** the change, using catalytic mechanisms.

In other words, we could choose to manage it as a project, in the way that many companies have done with regard to health and safety. We could lead it, by setting an example from the top as to what kinds of behaviour are to be emulated. Or we could nudge it into being, designing triggers that play to people's needs, motives and values. Thus, in the case of an experimental culture, it can be brought into being through plans, people or pointers.

In the remainder of this chapter, we shall use examples to examine each of these very different techniques.

1. Managing the change

The folklore of management

What first comes to mind when you think of management as an organizing principle? Does it lift your spirits and gladden your heart?

Almost all change management models follow roughly the same pattern. Set the goal, describe it with precision and invest it with passion. Bring people on board, make it a test of loyalty and build solidarity. Plot the journey to victory, chunk it up into bite-sized pieces and establish the milestones. Assign people to tasks, hold them accountable and challenge them to excel. Track their progress, reward them if they succeed and admonish them if they fail.

Perhaps the best known and certainly the most popular model is that of John Kotter, a professor at Harvard Business School. It manages change as an eight-stage process:

1 Create a sense of urgency.

2 Build a guiding coalition.

3 Form a strategy, vision and initiatives.

4 Enlist a volunteer army.

5 Enable action by removing barriers.

6 Generate short-term wins.

7 Sustain acceleration.

8 Institute change.

Kotter's model was well received because it recognized the importance of barriers to change, such as complacency, procrastination and passivity. It focused squarely on purpose, motivation and determination. And yet, for all its virtues, it still feels marooned in a world of authoritarian, almost militaristic, values and assumptions. It seems to assume most people feel somewhat helpless and dependent, and that success in business is a reward for effort, discipline and alignment. It makes business feel like a slog. In short, it is the language, not of experimentation, but of planning.

In common with most strategies for change, Kotter's model remained steeped in the ideology of management as a social technology for controlling and coordinating large numbers of people. We can think of these beliefs as the 'six pillars' of management, each based upon a (somewhat fragile) assumption. Yet, ever since Elton Mayo and the Human Relations School of management challenged these assumptions in the 1930s, there have been many voices arguing that managerialism rests on a flawed understanding of human nature. A very different perspective on each of these six pillars can be taken. Table 11.1 describes the contrasting views.

TABLE 11.1 Contrasting perspectives on management

Six pillars of management	Kotter (managerialism)	Elton Mayo (human relations)
Hierarchy of power	Order and efficiency are best achieved in an authoritarian structure.	*Crowd wisdom*, or more generally *collective intelligence*, is the theory that, for many classes of problem, many minds are wiser than one, however gifted that one person may be; in the long run, democracy outperforms autocracy.
Singularity of goal	Organizations perform at their best when their members are loyal to a common objective.	*Obliquity* is the principle that, in business as well as in life, we rarely get what we aim for and that many goals are best achieved indirectly; the art is to discover the oblique objective that, if pursued diligently, leads to our true goal.
Planning of outcomes	Objectives are best pursued by everyone following a predetermined schedule of activities.	*Emergent strategy* is the recognition that we discover the best means to a desired outcome less by deliberation than by allowing unexpected events to shape our actions; improvisation in the light of an unfolding reality more than compensates for our lack of clairvoyance.
Specialization of process	Jobs are best designed and performed if they are scaled to the individual employee.	The *silo mentality* is a direct outcome of chunking up the business into one-person-sized pieces of accountability called 'jobs'; most tasks are better performed by teams than individuals.

(continued)

TABLE 11.1   (Continued)

Six pillars of management	Kotter (managerialism)	Elton Mayo (human relations)
Standardization of process	There is a right way to do things and, in most aspects of business, the right way is already broadly understood.	*Best practice* is the myth that there are formulaic solutions to business problems that, if adopted, assure success; this is equivalent to believing that painting-by-numbers can produce great art.
Incentivization of money	Most people are motivated, more than anything else, by financial inducements.	Intrinsic motivation is the idea that the greatest satisfaction of doing a job well comes not from the material rewards of doing so but from the sheer pleasure of the activity itself; people cannot be bribed to give of their best.

The question is this: which of these sets of assumptions is closer to the truth? Or what other assumptions about effective work practices might be made? Or, indeed, can we assume that there are *any* universal answers to these questions? The important point is that only experimentation can point us to the truth. And this, of course, is the core message of this book. If we want management to be a rational activity, we have no alternative but to test our assumptions as rigorously as we can.

Here we have a paradox. In building a culture of experimentation, does it make sense to do so by managing our way to this post-managerial state of affairs? Can we use hierarchy to dismantle hierarchy, be bureaucratic in cutting bureaucracy, and adopt change management techniques to change management itself?

This is what makes building an experimental culture unique. It is not just another project or change initiative. It is deeper than that. It is the wholesale replacement of one mindset by another.

Limitations of the managerial model

There are three reasons why, perhaps, management is an inappropriate tool for creating a more experimental culture.

The **first reason** is that each of the six pillars of management is incompatible with experimentation, or at least would act as a barrier to the creation of an experimental culture:

- **Hierarchy of power** deprives the organization of the fullest access to the creative talents of its members, by assuming that a person's imaginative ability is a correlate of their seniority within the company.

- **Singularity of goal** produces the groupthink and inauthentic solidarity that inhibit the 'creative tension' and fearless dialogue that are the oxygen of an experimental culture.

- **Planning of outcomes,** like rain dancing, feeds the illusion that the future can be willed into action, thus supplanting the need for empirical research and radically reducing the relevance of experimentation.

- **Specialization of task** curbs the cross-boundary interaction that is fundamental if a culture of speculation and testing is to flourish.

- **Standardization of process** removes from discussion and debate the natural targets of any genuinely experimental culture.

- **Incentivization by money** taps into too small a part of what truly motivates people to invest their talent and goodwill in building an unfamiliar culture, with all its attendant risks.

The **second reason** for questioning a managerial approach is that it is failing even on its own terms. Consider the following three cases:

- Trevor Phillips, a British writer and former politician, wrote in October 2020 that, in 1922, 'London presided over a quarter of humanity (…) our government consisted of some 40,000 individuals including those in the colonial service – one civil servant for each 11,000 subjects. Today there is one for every 162 citizens and that's without counting the 300,000 in arm's-length bodies or the army who operate under banners of consultancy and outsourcing firms.'[3] Phillips asks the rhetorical, but relevant, question: 'How is it that we could rule Mumbai, Mombasa and Montserrat with quill pens but now, with quantum computers, can't even seem to handle sending masks to Manchester?'

- John Kearon, founder of Brainjuicer Group, argues that the adoption of 'marketing science' and 'the drive for short-term shareholder value' are the main reasons why large companies seem incapable of inventing the new brand categories that gave them their original success. He gives the example of Unilever. Roughly 70 per cent of its profits are made by brands that created the category in which they remain the brand leader, such as Persil washing powder, Birds Eye frozen foods, Comfort clothes conditioner, Cif non-abrasive cleaner, Dove moisturizing soap, Impulse body spray, and Magnum hand-held ice cream. Most of these brand categories were invented **before** the adoption of marketing science and innovation centres. Since then, Unilever, in common with most other large consumer products companies, would seem to have lost the ability to 'originate the sort of new category brands that deliver the majority of the company's profits'. Nearly all new categories are created by startups. The reason Kearon gives for this failure is the mindset of 'consumer led, trend led, image driven, think big, act big, avoid failure, avoid controversy, please shareholders, and look before you leap', all of which bear the stamp of managerialism.[4]

- In their research studies, Gary Hamel and Michele Zanini claimed that 'an excess of bureaucracy costs the U.S. economy more than $3 trillion annually (or 17 per cent of GNP)' and that 'in recent years, that tariff has been growing'.[5] These findings have been reinforced by a Deloitte study of the Australian economy in 2014 that showed that 8.9 million worker-years, or roughly $480 billion, are lost to the economy from what they call unnecessary 'paper-pushing' and 'bureaucratic busywork'.[6] Bureaucracy operates like a ratchet: it is always easier to add complexity than subtract it.

Managerialism would seem to be a broken technology. Can it really be relied upon to correct its own deficiencies?

The **third reason** builds on this argument. Is it rational to believe that managerial methods are able to build a post-managerial culture, despite their shortcomings when faced by much simpler tasks? Does it really make sense to appoint a project management team to dismantle the pillars of management?

In building an experimental culture, the things we most need to change are the assumptions that underpin managerialism. These can only be changed from a perspective outside management. So, instead of management, should we be placing our trust in *leadership*, and relying upon a remarkable individual who, by force of example, can inaugurate a more experimental culture? This then leads us to the second of our three techniques – influencing culture through leading change.

2. Leading the change

The exemplary leader

Leaders make things happen by example rather than instruction. They do not need the apparatus of a bureaucracy or a grand title to exert an influence. Their power derives not from their positional authority but from the force of their character. What power they possess comes by permission from those they lead. People find themselves imitating the behaviour of the leader. Looking upon the leader as an exemplar, they act their way into the person they become. This process has been called mimetic learning.

In the ancient world, everyone was brought up to study and emulate the lives of heroic individuals. One of the key texts was Plutarch's *Lives*. This hugely influential book, written in the 2nd century AD, told the stories of 48 extraordinary men. So well studied was it that Plutarch earned the title 'Teacher of Europe'.

What he taught was that the power of these great men did not flow from their position in society or from the authority vested in them. Rather, it found expression in their day-to-day conduct. In particular, it was conveyed by the virtues they chose to cultivate and embody, such as courage, piety or justice. It did not require the giving of orders or the control of activities or the expectation of obedience. The leader's role was to inspire others to find within themselves the will and desire to lead lives of virtue. Albert Schweitzer, a physician and humanitarian, argued that, 'Example is not the main thing in influencing others; it is the only thing.'[7]

The role of the leader, or the leadership team, is not to set strategy for others to execute but to create an environment in which those who need to make it happen share in the creation of such a culture. If the particular role of the leader is to inspire the creation of an experimental culture within the business, that leader will need to be an exemplary experimentalist.

Where might we find such a person? We need to find someone who deeply understands experimentation and who has led a successful experimental culture. Accordingly, we will examine the life and style of perhaps the greatest leader of a scientific laboratory in the 20th century, with more Nobel Prizes to its name than any other.

Max Perutz as an exemplary leader

In 1947, Max Perutz co-founded the Medical Research Council (MRC) Unit of Molecular Biology at the Cavendish Laboratory of Cambridge University. In 1962, he won the Nobel Prize in Chemistry, together with John Kendrew, for discovering the protein structure of haemoglobin. In the same year, he founded the Laboratory of Molecular Biology (LMB) at Cambridge, which he ran until 1979 and in which he worked until the end of his life in 2002.

During his tenure, the LMB was home to nine Nobel Prizes (shared among 13 scientists), four Orders of Merit and nine Copley Medals (the highest honour awarded by the Royal Society). Francis Crick, the discoverer, with James Watson, of the structure of DNA, said of Perutz that he had been at the heart of the revolution in molecular biology for 40 years.

What was his secret? This is how he described his principles:

> Choose outstanding people and give them intellectual freedom; show genuine interest in everyone's work, and give younger colleagues public credit; enlist skilled support staff who can design and build sophisticated and advanced new apparatus and instruments; facilitate the interchange of ideas, in the canteen as much as in seminars; have no secrecy; be in the laboratory most of the time and accessible to everybody where possible; and engender a happy environment where people's morale is kept high.[8]

He led by example. Despite being chairman of the LMB, he would spend almost all his time at the bench working alongside his fellow scientists. Over lunch in the canteen that his wife, Gisela, had designed as the nucleus of the lab, he would keep abreast of the work of his colleagues. Cesar Milstein, one of his most illustrious students, said of him: 'I learned what research was all about... I always received an unspoken message, which in my imagination I translated as, "Do good experiments and don't worry about the rest."'[9] Perutz declined a knighthood on the grounds that his young research staff might feel inhibited talking to him.

He distrusted bureaucracy. He preferred to lead through conversation and intimacy than rules and procedures. He expressed his philosophy forcefully:

> Creativity in science, as in the arts, cannot be organized. It arises
> spontaneously from individual talent. Well run laboratories can
> foster it, but hierarchical organization, inflexible bureaucratic rules
> and mountains of futile paperwork can kill it. Discoveries cannot be
> planned; they pop up, like Puck, in unexpected places.[10]

With regard to his distaste for planning, he once said: 'I rarely plan my research; it plans me.'[11]

Sari Nusseibeh, a philosopher and friend of Perutz, remarked that these noble principles for how a research lab should be run contrast strongly with the bureaucratic methods advocated by what he called 'the Paladins of accountability' in various funding and research councils, and increasingly by university administrators.[12] This book is written in the belief that this remains the case; indeed, it may well be getting worse.

In the same spirit, Sir James Black, a fellow Nobel Prize winner, described the culture that his friend had created in this pithy statement: 'No politics, no committees, no reports, no referees, no interviews – just highly motivated people picked by a few men of good judgment.'[13]

As a consequence, the LMB attracted many of the most gifted young scientists, all of whom were drawn to the lab by Perutz's humanity. His warmth, vitality and integrity were legendary. Such was his moral courage, for example, that, early in his career, he resigned from his lectureship at Cambridge in protest against what he regarded as wrong-headed decisions made by senior administrators in the university. Nusseibeh said that he 'combined, in a singular fashion, all the noblest instincts of mankind'.[14]

Last but not least, he had a passionate concern for the truth. He strongly rejected the view, advocated by post-structuralist philosophers among others, that scientific truth is a relative concept, inescapably biased by the subjectivity of the scientist. He would quote the words of his distinguished namesake, Max Planck:

> There is a real world independent of our senses: the laws of nature were not invented by man but forced upon him by that natural world. They are the expression of a rational order.[15]

Limitation of the leadership model

Sadly, for the world, for every Max Perutz there are many self-styled leaders who suck the energy out of the organization they profess to lead. In contrast to Perutz, whom one of his co-researchers described as 'a humane scientist who used his brilliance to illuminate and not to dazzle others', many leaders fall victim to pride, if not narcissism. They resort to eliciting followership rather than agency from their 'flock'. They take on the mantle of 'the great leader' and assume sole responsibility for the direction of the enterprise and the manner of its achievement. In so doing they often sap the organization of its self-confidence and creative energy.

Leadership all too easily lapses into management, and the hierarchical practices that accompany it. Without perhaps meaning to do so, leaders engender, if only by their own treatment of others, an instrumental culture in which individuals are treated as means to an end, and not as ends in themselves. Relationships become no more than transactions. Performance is reduced to an accounting calculation. Leaders who rely for their leadership upon their positional power betray the meaning of true leadership and forfeit their right to be perceived as leaders.

Cultural change is rarely led effectively from the top, if only because this was the culture that gave people their route to the top. This is the only culture they understand, and with which they naturally empathize. Only rarely will it be a culture that cultivates the experimental mindset. So if managing the change and leading the change have their limitations, what can be done? Let us turn to our final technique.

3. Catalysing the change

The concept of choice architecture

Whereas a leader influences behaviour directly, the choice architect does so indirectly. 'Choice architecture' is the term invented by Richard Thaler and Carl Sunstein to denote the way in which decisions may be influenced by the purposeful design of the context in which they are made. At a trivial level, for example, supermarkets place their most popular and profitable merchandise at eye level so as to promote its purchase. More profoundly, organ donation rates are enhanced if people are required to opt out if they are unwilling to do so, rather than opt in. On a much grander scale, democratic institutions create civil societies. Thaler and Sunstein describe such 'nudges' as 'any aspect of the choice architecture that alters people's behaviour in a predictable way without forbidding any options or significantly changing their economic incentives'.[16] Thus, a nudge is not a directive. It still leaves room for freedom of choice.

In a managerial setting, the art of nudging people towards beneficial outcomes is clearly an important skill. The choice architect will want to manipulate the critical contextual variables so as to nudge behaviour towards desired outcomes. If the goal, for example, is to minimize the short-term bias of your shareholders, then, as Colin Mayer, a finance professor, has recommended, the voting rights of shareholders should be reserved only for those who hold their shares for a minimum period of time, such as two years.[17] But what if the goal is to increase the use of experimentation as a managerial tool in a large corporation? What kind of choice architecture will achieve this objective?

The short answer is that each of the critical business processes will need to be designed to elicit and reinforce experimental behaviour. This has been called a process of congruence, whereby the 'fitness variables' are brought into alignment with each other and, more importantly, with experimentation as a critical part of the manager's job. An experimental culture will be very different from a traditional managerial culture.

Every company is composed of a rather small number of 'fitness variables' that together constitute the culture of the organization and are critical to the well-being of the firm. These are five of the most important:

- how decisions are made;
- who gets recruited and promoted;
- what rules are followed;
- how time is allocated;
- what is measured and evaluated.

If they work well individually – and, more importantly, if they work well together in the service of a shared objective – the performance of the firm is enhanced. But if this objective changes, it follows as night follows day that the 'settings' of these fitness variables will need to be adjusted to align with the new objective. In changing the culture of an organization, the answers to these five big questions will have to change. For example, if the organization is to shift from one based on control to one based on learning, this will be the guiding criterion for each of the fitness variables. What if the predominant desire of the company is to transform its culture from one of managerialism (based on the orderly logic of hierarchy and bureaucracy) to one of experimentation (based on the evolutionary logic of variation and selection)? How would the fitness variables have to change to become congruent with this ambition? And what method can be used to stimulate the change? If not management or leadership, then what exactly?

Catalytic mechanisms

Almost every organization practises management-by-objective. Every strategic plan opens with a vision statement. Every management team is expected to have a goal. This is fine, but it has its dangers. Objectives lead inexorably to plans, budgets, key performance indicators and benchmarks. And plans come attached to processes, standard operating procedures and the whole apparatus of implementation. Before you know it, the firm is mired in bureaucracy. Little wonder that over 70 per cent of change programmes fail to deliver.

There is an alternative. Instead of bureaucracy, there are 'catalytic mechanisms', defined by Jim Collins, a Stanford professor of business, as 'non-bureaucratic devices that translate lofty aspirations into concrete reality'.[18]

A relatively trivial example of a catalytic mechanism (CM) would be a clock in a meeting room that told, not the time, but the *cost* of the meeting. Given the number of people in the meeting and their pay grade, it would record and display the escalating cost. In no way is the clock part of the corporate bureaucracy, but it would undoubtedly have an influence on the length and productivity of meetings in its presence. It would be 'nudging' the members of the meeting to use their time well.

A more dramatic example of a CM would be to disband the strategic planning process whereby an executive board allocates capital to each of its strategic business units, often on the basis of their projected financial performance. Instead, each business unit would be given the right, and responsibility, to raise its own funds on the capital markets, and on whatever terms it negotiated. This act of empowerment would reduce bureaucracy. Its catalytic effect would probably be to liberate the entrepreneurial talent of the business units.

Any effective catalytic mechanism works as a choice architecture. It operates 'at arm's length'. It is designed to influence behaviour indirectly. It nevertheless can impact performance dramatically. Replacing a corporate hierarchy with an internal market offers a dramatic example. For example, what if the performance of each business in the company were treated like horses in a race and became part of a betting market open to all employees in the business? Wouldn't it be interesting to see how each business was priced by employees collectively gambling on the future performance of the company they know so well? Wouldn't it also be interesting to discover how the employees' predictions differed from those of the executive board, and then to discover whose forecasts were the more accurate?

Choice architecture on a grand scale

Some of the most exciting and profound experiments in business make use of choice architectures very different from the normal design of a business, such as a betting market, or an auction, or an internal capital market. This method offers a dramatic route whereby a rather traditional organization can test non-managerial ways of organizing work and competing for customers. We shall describe two choice architectures to illustrate their power: one relating to the growth of civilization, and the other to the impact of urbanization.

CASE STUDY 1
Civilization

Historians have long wondered why it was that at the start of the 16th century Western Europe began its seemingly remorseless climb to world domination, not only economically but also culturally. In effect, the modern world was invented in this small corner of the world, and with it, the unparalleled advances in humanity's knowledge, longevity and enjoyment of life. Charles Murray, a political scientist, has calculated that 72 per cent of the 'significant figures' in art and science between 1400 and 1950 came from just four countries in the world: France, Italy, Germany and Britain.[19] How can this be explained? What was unique about Europe? Niall Ferguson, a Scottish-American historian, provides the following explanation. He describes what he calls six 'killer apps' – or social developments – as the main causes of this remarkable phenomenon:[20]

- **Competition:** Europe's patchwork quilt of independent nations (effectively, city states) stimulated intense mutual rivalry and expanded their interests and trade across the world. By contrast, China was a single, monolithic society focused strongly on its internal well-being and the joys of stability and permanence.

- **Consumption:** The increase in global trade and the fascination with exotic products whet the appetite for material possessions and the habit of acquisition, creating a virtuous spiral of production and consumption. The market, as a fundamental institution, became the engine of exchange, both of commodities and ideas.

- **Science:** The rediscovery of classical civilization and a consequent renaissance of learning, stimulated by the invention of the printing press, caused a dramatic growth in literacy, curiosity and experimental science. By contrast, the Islamic world, after its extraordinary golden age, fell victim to a form of clericism that smothered the spirit of inquiry.

- **Medicine:** The success and development of the scientific method, along with a newfound belief in rational thought, led to dramatic developments in medicine, health and longevity.

- **Property:** The development of democratic institutions, such as widely distributed property rights and the rule of law, had the effect of turning serfs into citizens, and empowering very large numbers of people to direct their own lives and cultivate their own interests. The values of the Enlightenment were one of the results.

- **Work ethic:** The Christian faith, and particularly Protestantism, was unique among religions in placing so much emphasis on the sanctity of work (and the sin of idleness). The Protestant work ethic became a powerful force in driving the industrial revolution and the fervour with which it was conducted.

Each of these 'killer apps' acted as a **choice architecture**. Working in combination, they formed a particular setting or ambience that was favourable to the development of modern civilization. In other words, the explanation for the achievements of 'the West' had nothing to do with the genetic character of the individuals who happened to inhabit this part of the world, but everything to do with the environment in which they found themselves. The killer apps nudged people in certain directions: Protestantism towards an ethic of hard work; trade and commerce towards an appetite for possessions; cross-cultural mixing towards an aptitude for creativity; and individualism towards a taste for self-expression.

In short, the challenge to any particular business lies less in the choice of people to recruit and retain and more in the **choice architecture** – or *killer app* – that it designs to bring out the best in those that it already employs. An equally important challenge is to use experimentation to discover just such a choice architecture.

CASE STUDY 2
Cities

Jane Jacobs, an urban activist, was intrigued by how to explain the vibrancy of the neighbourhood in which she lived – Greenwich Village in New York. It is a tiny part of Lower Manhattan but has always been a fountain of culture. She likened it to a 'spontaneous ballet' of school kids, homemakers and entrepreneurs interacting spontaneously with each other and comprising a dynamic community. In *The Death and Life of Great American Cities*, she championed in particular the 'surplus of human capital' that seemed to accompany a neighbourhood characterized by sidewalks, parks, older buildings, short blocks, local economies, mixed-use buildings and a diverse citizenry.[21]

Geoffrey West, a mathematician, sought to translate Jacobs' intuitive concepts into mathematical laws about how urban environments stimulate civilized living, and therefore how they might be designed purposefully to enhance cultural productivity.[22] What he discovered was that the *per capita* productivity of a city increases by 15 per cent for every doubling of population. So, for example, if a city of 250,000 grows to half a million, its inhabitants should expect to earn 15 per cent more in salary or, in the case of inventors, to register 15 per cent more patents. Related to this law is the finding that density also matters. The more that people 'bump into' each other – the greater the 'urban friction' – the more energized and creative the neighbourhood becomes.

West expected to find parallels between cities and corporations. But he was surprised – and dismayed – to find just the opposite. As companies grow, they become *less* productive and *less* profitable per employee. It is as though size and scale act to demote creativity and dampen innovation. They do this by reducing the 'collisions' between people. The urge to control who works *for* whom and *with* whom means that hierarchies get built, barriers get created and silos get installed. Boxes replace bridges. The result is that conversation suffers, and networks shrink. The obsession with efficiency displaces a passion for innovation.

Some firms are bucking the trend. In common with many other firms, GSK, for example, has built a new office complex at the Navy Yard in Philadelphia that works very much to West's principles. It comprises a large atrium from which at least one-third of the workforce can be seen, and around which large numbers of employees can serendipitously bump into each other, emulating the urban friction that is the source of a city's cultural pizzazz.

Two examples of choice architecture in business

Both of the following case histories employ the paradigm of the market as the favoured choice architecture.

CASE STUDY 3
The shadow organization

This was a London Business School experiment that we designed in conjunction with the learning and development team at a French electric utility company. Its purpose was to jump-start a big innovation drive within the company.

The idea was that the chief executive would invite a group of managers from all levels, functions and business units to each put forward a single problem to which the solution would, in their opinion, contribute most to the performance of the company. This newly formed 'shadow organization' would then democratically select from among these problems the critical few that they felt to be particularly important. Breaking into small teams, and released entirely from their 'day jobs', they would then work on their problem, using experimentation as the principal means of solving the issue.

In effect, the shadow organization, numbering several hundred managers, would become an alternative way of doing business and the prototype of a wholly new, experimental way of tackling the company's issues. If successful, it would gradually replace the legacy organization.

CASE STUDY 4
The OpenMarket

This was another experiment we designed, but this time with a multinational French consumer products company. As with the shadow organization, it is based on bringing the market inside the firm, but in this case, it includes a market in financial capital as well as a market in ideas.

The idea was that several small groups of managers would be bankers, and others would be entrepreneurs. The banks would be well funded, and would be given the objective, in competition with each other, to lend to those entrepreneurial teams whose ideas they favoured as having the greatest potential. The entrepreneurs, also in small teams, would compete to attract funds from the banks.

In effect, an internal market would be created that could test the viability of bringing the virtues (and vices) of competition within the organization. It would be a bold experiment in the radical transformation of a hierarchy into what has been called an individualized corporation.[23]

In Appendix F, we reproduce the format in which the full experimental designs of both the 'shadow organization' and the 'OpenMarket' were first described and presented within their respective companies.

Summary

Traditional methods of change management, directed from the top, have a patchy record of achievement. Experimentation offers an alternative. We have proposed three broad approaches to doing so – by management, by leadership and by choice architecture. There is no decisive evidence one way or the other as to which of these three models (or any others that can be invented) works best. Indeed, the answer may be specific to the situation, with no formulaic solution or 'best practice' to hand.

Each organization must find its own truth. So, our conclusion is this: use experimentation to test which experimental culture works best in your own organization. Build your own idiosyncratic architecture. Make your own discoveries. In the next chapter we describe how.

Notes

1 Pfeffer, J and Sutton, R I (2006) *Hard Facts, Dangerous Half-Truths and Total Nonsense: Profiting from evidence-based management*, Harvard Business School Press, Boston

2 Goddard, J (20 November 2014) The fatal bias, www.london.edu/think/the-fatal-bias (archived at https://perma.cc/JM9D-SKR7); and Raynor, M and Ahmed, M (April 2013) Three rules for making a company truly great, *Harvard Business Review*

3 Phillips, T (19 October 2020) Burnham exposes the sorry state we're in, *The Times*, www.thetimes.co.uk/article/burnham-exposes-the-sorry-state-were-in-wz66t6gsq (archived at https://perma.cc/Q3T9-EPRZ)

4 www.marketingsociety.com/the-library/death-innovation (archived at https://perma.cc/2YC5-77HN)

5 Hamel, G and Zanini, M (16 May 2017) Assessment: Do you know how bureaucratic your organization is?, *Harvard Business Review*, hbr.org/2017/05/assessment-do-you-know-how-bureaucratic-your-organization-is (archived at https://perma.cc/X7NZ-TPWS)

6 Deloitte (2014) Get out of your own way: Unleashing productivity, www2.deloitte.com/content/dam/Deloitte/au/Documents/Building%20Lucky%20Country/deloitte-au-btlc-get-out-your-own-way-230217.pdf (archived at https://perma.cc/3NNY-VSER)

7 Schweitzer, A and Mellon Jr, W L (1996) *Brothers in Spirit*, Syracuse University Press, New York

8 Thomas, J M (2004) Max Perutz, 19 May 1914 – 6 February 2002, *Proceedings of the American Philosophical Society*, **148** (2)

9 www.goodreads.com/author/quotes/7827095.C_sar_Milstein (archived at https://perma.cc/S3Q3-X5WY)

10 McKie, R (5 August 2007) So what if he was afraid of bananas?, *The Observer*, www.theguardian.com/books/2007/aug/05/biography.features1 (archived at https://perma.cc/2AYR-GVLD)

11 quotefancy.com/quote/1554500/Max-Perutz-I-rarely-plan-my-research-it-plans-me (archived at https://perma.cc/LS7M-VM94)

12 Tribute paid to Max Perutz prior to the Max Perutz Memorial Lecture given by Professor Sari Nusseibeh at the International Human Rights Network of Academics and Scholarly Societies, Royal Society, London, 19 May 2005.

13 Sir James Black, quoted in Jack, A (1 February 2009) An acute talent for innovation, *Financial Times*

14 Tribute paid to Max Perutz prior to the Max Perutz Memorial Lecture given by Professor Sari Nusseibeh at the International Human Rights Network of Academics and Scholarly Societies, Royal Society, London, 19 May 2005.

15 Max Planck, *The Philosophy of Science*, quoted in Perutz, M (2002) *I Wish I'd Made You Angry Earlier: Essays on science, scientists and humanity*, Cold Spring Harbor Press, Cold Spring Harbor, NY

16 Thaler, R H and Sunstein, C R (2008) *Nudge: Improving decisions about health, wealth and happiness*, Yale University Press, New Haven, CT

17 Mayer, C (2013) *Firm Commitment: Why the corporation is failing us and how to restore trust in it*, Oxford University Press, Oxford

18 Collins, J (July–August 1999) Turning goals into results: The power of catalytic mechanisms, *Harvard Business Review*

19 Murray, C (2004) *Human Accomplishment: The pursuit of excellence in the arts and sciences, 800 BC to 1950*, HarperCollins, New York

20 Ferguson, N (2012) *Civilization: The West and the rest*, Penguin Books, London

21 Jacobs, J (1993) *The Death and Life of Great American Cities*, Vintage Books, London

22 West, G (2017) *Scale: The universal laws of life and death in organisms, cities and companies*, Penguin Books, London

23 Ghoshal, S and Bartlett, C A (1998) *The Individualized Corporation: A fundamentally new approach to management*, William Heinemann, London

12

Experimentation:
A catalyst for change

As we began the experiment review meeting with our Paris-based clients, we were feeling hesitant. Months earlier, we had spoken with the team of financial services executives about experimentation. At the time, they had seen it as a diversion from their main priority of getting sales figures back on track. However, with some caution, they eventually decided to adopt an experimental approach to that particular problem. They ring-fenced their southwest locations as the experiment 'test site', while using more traditional ways of enhancing sales performance in the other regions.

As we began to speak, our earlier concerns were immediately lifted. It was clear that the room was buzzing with energy as they recounted the impact of the experiment. Yes… the experiment had improved sales and the new process tested by the experiment could be rolled out in the other regions, but the excitement was about much more than that. The team had been surprised by the way in which their people had embraced the whole idea of experimentation. By dispensing with hierarchies, by empowering people to be involved in the decision-making, by encouraging ideas and creating greater ownership as part of the experiment process, they were startled by the reactions. One of the team said, 'It's almost like a different culture in the southwest now.' Another remarked how those involved had told her: 'We never want to go back to the old ways.'

Thus began a discussion that we have had many times. The French team , like others that have experienced such transformations, wanted to know how best to build upon their success. Questions we often hear are:

- What is the best way of sharing this experience beyond our own functions?
- How can you even start to transform a corporate culture?
- How do you move from one set of processes, values and attitudes to another?
- What best induces individuals to alter their ways of working, thinking and acting?

In previous chapters we have provided guidance for the experimentalist that focuses on their immediate environment. This has ranged from personal experiments to guidance for the intrapreneur where topics and outcomes are closely related to their own business function. Such experiments are more contained and the successes more localized. It is when the experimentalist wants to influence the wider organization, to mobilize others and champion the benefits of experimentation, that the questions above arise.

It might be argued that there is no better vehicle to influence culture change than experimentation. Like our French clients, after their first experience, many are inspired to go on and seek even more ways of doing things differently. We have taken the frequently asked questions above and reformatted them to explain more about how culture change can happen:

1 How can we share this experience beyond our own functions?
2 How can you start to transform a corporate culture?

 o How do you move one set of processes, values and attitudes to another?

 o How can individuals alter their ways of working, thinking and acting?

We suggest that an initial focus on the first question provides the platform for a 'nudge' approach to achieving the second.

It reinforces our argument that cultural change can be best achieved by the use of catalytic mechanisms that influence behaviour in an indirect way. In this case we use the experiment experience itself as a catalyst for wider organizational change.

We also propose that changing organizational culture in a sustainable way involves an incremental approach working across the organization rather than relying on a single top-driven, 'big bang' approach.

The following sections describe ways in which experimentation can be used as a catalyst to support culture change:

1 *The continuing challenges;*

2 *The experiment experience as a platform for change;*

3 *Six ways to create an experimental culture;*

4 *Getting the best from a top–down approach;*

5 *Randstad case study (Appendix G).*

1. The continuing challenges – what *still* concerns us

Changing entrenched habits and behaviours in established organizations is never going to be easy. Earlier in the book we explained why the time is right for more innovative ways of working as organizations recalibrate their business models and operating processes after the pandemic. That continues to be true but it comes with a health warning as this shift should not be mistaken for an open door to experimentation. Some of the traditional obstacles remain and those we highlight here are ones that we observe as continuing concerns when working with clients.

Hidden cultures

We described in earlier chapters that the true measure of how receptive an organization is in encouraging an experimental approach is usually hidden. It is the underlying, unstated culture of how the business actually operates that tells the real story, rather than

PR-slanted declarations of 'fostering innovation and creativity'. It is reflected in the degree to which senior managers tolerate failure and risk-taking and how they champion innovative ideas. In simple terms, it is what organizations and the people within them *do* rather than what they *say*. Too often we see the 'innovation' rhetoric concealing the underlying culture of an organization. When faced with short-term operational challenges, we continue to see organizations reverting to the control loop and previous solutions to problems rather than sticking to their stated beliefs and aspirations of an innovative approach.

Increasing bureaucracy

Despite the impression that organizations are becoming flatter and less bureaucratic, Gary Hamel and Michele Zanini's survey of *Harvard Business Review* members in 2017[1] found the opposite. More recent events will have had an impact, but at that time, nearly two-thirds of 7,000 respondents felt that their organization had become even *more* bureaucratic over the last few years. From an experimentation perspective, 80 per cent said that new ideas were likely to encounter indifference or resistance. A huge 96 per cent of those in larger organizations did not feel supported in launching even small-scale experiments. There is still a long way to go for experimentalists if they want to overcome these increasing constraints.

Disconnected performance measures

Performance measures are an essential part of any business – try managing without them. Inevitably, they play a critical role in driving behaviours and attitudes that underpin the organizational culture. And yet... when developing an organizational culture to support experimentation, they are rarely adjusted and their impact can be frequently overlooked altogether. In Chapter 6, we described the ways in which 'traditional' management practices can become irrelevant or even counterproductive in an experimental culture. However, we continue to see organizations measuring individual performance on exactly those behaviours. We frequently hear businesses talking, with genuine intent, about their aims of 'promoting innovation' or 'encouraging creativity'. Yet... when we observe the competences on which they measure, and reward, individuals in annual performance reviews, too often they promote rigidity and stifle innovation.

Busyness not business

One of the biggest challenges we continue to observe among potential experimentalists, and managers generally, is the ability to create time to step back and think. Busyness has almost become a status symbol in today's business world, where the demands on managers' time means that time to think is a rarity. How many times do you hear someone in the workplace respond 'busy' when asked how they are? We now have more 'productivity' tools and more ways to communicate than ever before and, rather than ease things, they place even more pressure on people's time and accessibility. As people run from meeting to meeting, attack the inbox or work on the next deliverable, they rarely take time to pause and think about the bigger picture or new and different ways of doing things.

The message for the experimentalist is that, despite a newfound appeal for trying different ways of working, changing established practices is never easy. That does not mean that it cannot be done. In the next sections we suggest ways to make it happen.

2. The experiment as a platform for change

To provide context for the following sections, we begin by making a number of assumptions. First, we expect you to have already completed a business experiment with your own team and learned from its success. Second, we assume that the experiment was 'contained' within a discrete part of the business. Finally, we presume that you have an ambition to share your experience and widen the organizational impact and benefits of experimentation.

It is, of course, impossible to make every idea or suggestion relevant to every reader. Our aim is simply for everyone to benefit from at least some of the following suggestions. We want you to choose what is most relevant to your own situation and try out the ideas and tactics for yourself, your team and, ultimately, your organization.

You have already started!

As a reader of this book, you will almost certainly have started to answer the questions above – perhaps without realizing it. If, as we assume, you have completed a successful experiment, you are already on your way. You have an exemplar and experiences to share. The following points explain why the experiment itself can provide a foundation for change:

- **You have an ally**. In the intrapreneur's checklist in Chapter 5 we spoke of the importance of seeking senior-level sponsors. They will already be advocates of experimentation, particularly if it has brought measurable benefits.

- **You have a model**. In the same checklist, we suggested that you choose an experiment topic that can be replicated across functions and businesses. In this way a success in one area can be spread to others.

- **You have cultural 'targets'**. In Chapter 10 we defined the distinctive cultural practices of an experimental organization and asked you to assess your own organization against those characteristics. Thus, you already have an appreciation of where your organization is strong or weak on these criteria. We explained that it is rare for an organization not to have some weaknesses. So don't try to change everything at once. Select the behaviours or competencies that you particularly want to strengthen.

- **You know what to expect**. The cultural assessment will have provided a useful starting point. However, our message for the experimentalist aiming to spread the word is to beware of the 'hidden' culture and *begin* with a 'worst case' scenario. It means expecting that the business and the managers you encounter are highly risk-averse and that failure is not an option. It means assuming that time and resources are unlikely to be available. It means presuming that other senior managers may not be as enthusiastic as your experiment sponsor. Too often we have seen experiment teams buoyed by organizational rhetoric and the early enthusiasm of others, having to recalibrate, and sometimes even restart, their experiments when faced with later reluctance. Starting from a position of wariness will save much time and effort in the long run.

3. Creating an experimental culture

Having a successful experiment behind you, along with a core team of enthusiasts and a senior-level sponsor, is an enviable starting point. However, thinking that these factors alone are sufficient to influence the wider organization can be a mistake. This next section looks at six ways in which this can be achieved (Figure 12.1).

FIGURE 12.1   Six practical steps for creating an experimental culture

a. What you can do

As an advocate of change, you will clearly need to be a role model, and that starts with a self-assessment. The question that needs to be asked is: 'How much do I display the behaviours, values and attitudes that we want to encourage?' The word 'display' is an important part of the question. If others are to be influenced, they will need to see and feel the differences. You need to be *doing* something as evidence that things really are changing. Here are a few ideas that can help an individual manager:

- Revisit the personal assessment questionnaire. Having been through the experiment experience with others, how would you *now* score yourself? What are the competences that you can capitalize upon and what are the areas you now need to develop?

- Involve others in your development. Use the personal assessment questionnaire for informal 360 feedback. Ask a number of close colleagues to provide their feedback on your competences and see how closely they match your own.

- Undertake a personal experiment using the template provided and the results of the questionnaire. Explain to others what you are doing and why. Encourage them to do the same. We don't expect you to go as far as one senior client, who took his team of 80 people through a PowerPoint presentation of his own 360 report, including his developmental action plan. However, such transparency and 'vulnerability' lend themselves to an experimental environment where people feel free to question and support each other's development.

- Avoid busyness. Diarize (and ring-fence) an hour twice a week to create time to think more strategically – and experimentally. This does two things: it provides some space to elevate yourself above the daily operational concerns of the business; and it role-models the fact that busyness is not a reflection of importance or status.

- Take a fresh look at your environment. What are the physical factors that could be changed to make a positive statement that things are different? Among the 'nudge' tactics we have seen are such things as: adapting office layouts, stopping 'unnecessary' meetings, discarding unproductive processes and removing trappings of status.

• Personally encourage the behaviours you admire. This is not about blanket emails or public recognition – quite the opposite. It is when a manager, either personally (preferably) or by phone or email, congratulates an individual who has role-modelled the desired behaviour. In our experience, such informal messages are soon shared with others and the indirect, informal nature of the communication makes it, strangely, even more powerful.

b. Create a compelling story

The downloadable guides and earlier text that introduced the concepts and our approach to experimentation will play an important part in educating those unfamiliar with the process. However, they are unlikely to be as inspiring as the first few successful experiments conducted in the firm. Such experiences can become the source of compelling stories and act as a catalyst for change.

In an incremental approach to change, the obvious starting point for spreading the word will be in the business area of the original experiment. The core experiment team and those involved in that experiment will be familiar with the concepts and practices of experimentation, but it is likely that the wider population in that business area will not. Encouraging and creating opportunities for those involved in the original experiment to share their experiences will help to engage and educate the wider population about the new ways of working.

For managers, there may also be opportunities to involve peers from a cross-functional management team. Subsequent stages will target other business functions and seek more senior-level support to create a fuller organizational impact. Whatever the target level, if others are to be influenced, experimentation needs to be presented with a message that educates, informs and inspires.

Developing a narrative that will appeal to all levels in the business requires a combination of the logical language of the conscious mind with the emotional language of the unconscious mind. The message therefore needs to project a relevant and rational business case alongside a proposal that is both exciting and inspiring. The following format is not meant to be prescriptive and should be tailored as necessary, but it does reflect many of the tactics that we see being used successfully.

CREATING A COMPELLING STORY

1 Make the message value-centric or customer-centric – it's about the business.

2 Explain why experimentation can be an important tool. Highlight current problems or imminent opportunities that might benefit from the approach.

3 Describe the differences between experimentation and traditional practices. Explain the benefits, namely risk reduction, re-scoping and resource savings.

4 Explain the importance of the recently completed experiment topic. Detail the outcomes – exact figures of costs saved, revenue increased, and performance enhanced.

5 Extrapolate the outcomes to the scale of the company to demonstrate the potential impact of the experiment.

6 Identify what can be done in *other* parts of the businesses, how the original experiment could be replicated and how issues elsewhere could be resolved.

7 Involve those in the original core experiment team. Let them tell their stories in their own words with their own enthusiasm.

8 Use testimonials or video diaries of those in the experiment itself. How have they been influenced in the ways they work?

9 Use the sponsors to endorse the benefits of experimentation. A two-minute video clip can be an effective 'call to arms'.

10 Make it easy for others to start. Offer support and guidance. Use the materials in this book. If you want others to follow, they will need that guidance.

c. Spreading the message

For managers aiming to create an impact across the wider organization, we encourage them to consider a simple stakeholder mapping exercise. Using a 3x3 matrix with proponents, neutral and opponents on one axis and high, medium and low influencers on the other, it helps to target key players. Once the core message has been crafted, the stakeholder map can be supported by a communications plan that determines how, when and where it will be shared and by whom. This formalized approach to sharing the message is straight out of the 'normal' change management handbook and illustrates the points we made earlier. Experimentation is not change management, but it often applies the tools as part of the process.

The experiment sponsor can also be an important ally in providing access to their networks and help to implement the communication plan. Others have sought opportunities to provide short 'show and tell' briefings about the experiment experience in other parts of the business.

Many of those we have worked with are members of cross-functional management teams. They may not have been involved in the original experiment, so it provides another opportunity to share the learning. One group of senior executives in Canada were so convinced by the experimental outcomes of one of its members that they agreed to include experimentation in their annual objectives. As a group they committed to conduct two experiments per year that 'could add substantial value to the business'. In addition, each executive committed to conduct a separate experiment in their own business function as a way of further influencing the desired culture.

d. Create an experimental environment

We described the importance of role-modelling as an important part of creating an experimental culture. The following list provides some more tips and activities to support that process:

- Arrange for your immediate team (and others) to do the organization culture survey. Set up a session to share the results and gain a collective view of the strengths and weaknesses and where improvements need to be made.

- Create an initial framework of 'freedom' to experiment. It means giving people space to be playful and innovative but within some established boundaries. There is a danger that asking people to come up with innovative ideas will result in unrealistic proposals. At a later stage the whacky ideas may be exactly what you want to explore and the framework can then be expanded to encourage them. However, when starting out, it is useful to provide initial boundaries to corral the ideas. An example might be to propose that all the ideas should seek improvements within the frame of the 5Ps: people, productivity, processes, performance and profitability.

- Nudge people into finding the time. Send a 30-minute calendar invite to employees to respond to two operational questions, or come up with ideas in the 5P frame. Let them see that taking time to think and to experiment is an important part of the job.

- Set aside 30 minutes at the end of selected meetings to be dedicated to innovation and experimentation. We have seen this used effectively to review ideas and opportunities for experimentation.

- Build a new class of hero. This is where experimentalists can be publicly celebrated. Our health warning is that it should not be trivialized into an 'employee of the month' format. The reward or recognition needs to be sophisticated and sufficiently appealing to make others want to emulate the chosen 'hero'.

- Make a statement with the choice of performance measures. If there is the managerial capacity to do so, build in new metrics that encourage the desired behaviours and get rid of those that do not. Make sure people know why the changes are being made and inform them early on.

- Host short, informal breakfast sessions or lunch-and-learn events with small mixed-level groups on the topics of experimentation, innovation and new ways of working.

• Establish a community forum for knowledge-sharing and put it to work. There are too many discussion forums that simply dry up because they are underused. If a discussion forum is to be successful, it needs to be seen as an integral part of the 'new ways of working'. It needs to be attractive and purposeful for both contributors and readers to be drawn to it and to use it. Content that we have seen successfully used in these types of forum are:

  ○ a drop box for innovative ideas;

  ○ weekly meeting updates on the state of experimentation;

  ○ employees share their experimental experiences;

  ○ a weekly question about a particular experimental topic to prompt discussion;

  ○ shared resources, articles and academic papers with the latest research and news about experimentation;

  ○ insert short videos of innovation-related content, such as TED Talks.

e. Promote opportunities for experimentation

Place links to downloadable tools such as those provided in this book. Set up an online ideas forum using an established framework such as the 5Ps to create focus. The boundaries can also be set by framing questions such as, 'If you were the boss, what bureaucratic processes would you change and what alternatives might there be?' or 'What if we got rid of sales targets or performance reviews?'

Create a system for logging the ideas. Make it transparent to ensure that all the ideas are acknowledged and not forgotten or neglected. Using a system whereby ideas are submitted on a standard template encourages contributors to focus upon the business benefits of the idea and how the hypothesis might best be tested. A simple feedback mechanism to the originator to acknowledge their contribution acts as a token of appreciation.

Take a half-day to try something new to the business. Bring people together in a large group, split them into smaller groups, and use idea-generation techniques to address a particular problem or question, such as, 'How can we become more innovative?' The whackiest ideas can be encouraged. Everyone then shares the techniques they used and the potential solutions they generated. The resulting actions taken need to be fed back to the group.

f. Experiment with experimentation – just do it!

Each section above has tactics, tips and advice that will help the intrapreneur influence others in the organization. Clearly, not every tip or idea will be relevant in every situation. They are not meant to be. However, even those with less relevance often prompt further ideas that may well be relevant. There can be few better ways of sharing knowledge and promoting the benefits of experimentation than actually *doing* it. Here are some further tips from our experiences with other teams:

- Start small – do something simple. Experiments do not need to be complicated. They can be both fun and engaging, particularly if they challenge existing work practices. Some of the experiments we have worked with that fall into this category include exploring:
  - the impact of walking meetings;
  - efficiency improvements of stand-up meetings;
  - declaring an email-free day in the week;
  - working in peer-managed teams;
  - flexible working options;
  - reverse mentoring, such as graduates mentoring senior executives.

  Any experiment, even a small one, should use the proposal template to encourage people to use the six-step process or their own adaptation of it.

- Cascade the experiment experience… with an experiment! A business team we worked with in South America, made up of five managers from different functions, decided to cascade their experience in their own business areas. They each set up an experiment group and a control group in their individual functions and asked them to generate ideas for improving business performance. The experiment groups used the six-step process and the control groups used 'normal' idea-generation tools. It came as no surprise that the quantity and quality of ideas generated by the experiment groups were far superior to those of the control groups. But, while that was the main outcome, an additional benefit was that a wider population was exposed to the power of an experimental approach.

- Run experiments on key behaviours that support the desired culture. Many teams we have worked with, often frustrated by the attitudes to innovation, risk and failure, have run experiments on exactly those topics. The aim is to look at ways in which the organization can start to change its stance. These experiments are particularly relevant if tied to a collective assessment of the competences that need strengthening in the organization.

4. Getting the best from top–down

In this last chapter our focus has been on the way in which experimentation can be used as a catalyst for organizational change. That has meant providing managers and functional heads with tactics and tools to influence the organization beyond their own area of business. Yet, this is only part of the story of organizational change.

The degree to which experimentation succeeds as a catalyst for change will be dependent on a number of factors. In smaller organizations, led by a strong champion, we have seen it happen quickly and with enthusiasm. In other cases, particularly in larger, more hierarchical and bureaucratic structures, it will be a much slower process. In such cases, culture change may be confined to discrete parts of the business. Influencing the whole organization will take much longer as the barriers gradually fall. The competitive environment will also play a part in shaping the desire to change the way in which the organization operates. The point we make here is that experimentation can be a powerful catalyst for change, but, in larger organizations in particular, it will require greater impetus.

We have described how individual sponsors at a senior level who can communicate the lessons and benefits across the organization are key elements of an experimental approach. The real turning point is when the decision-makers themselves are influenced by these messages or, better still, decide independently that change needs to happen and that embracing such an approach would benefit the wider business.

It is when there is both top–down and bottom–up pressures to change that a winning combination is created. It is based on the premise that there is a clear and compelling business reason for change. Using that as a foundation, the organization can employ an experimental approach, along with other catalysts for change, to spread the philosophy downwards, upwards and across.

Throughout this book, we have stressed the point that the constraints of bureaucracy and managerialism mean that only rarely is lasting change led effectively from the top. This type of 'failure' is quoted frequently in the change management literature, but the definition of 'failure' can be contentious. A more reliable statistic is that 30 per cent of such initiatives are 'completely successful'. It means that many organizations *do* get it right and that a top–down approach can be one element in a successful initiative.

Appendix G provides an illustration of how an engaged leadership team, using a top–down approach to encourage experimentation, can accelerate the process of culture change in even the largest of global organizations.

Summary

This final chapter has been aimed at providing the individual intrapreneur with additional guidance to develop an experimental culture in their business. We began by sharing our concerns about the challenges that still abound and then introduced six ways in which they can be overcome. Clearly, not every activity or tip will be relevant in every situation, and we expect you to select what fits best for your situation – or perhaps be inspired to consider variations on similar themes. The principal focus throughout this chapter has been on how the individual can influence upwards and across the organization. In the book, we have been critical of managerialism and bureaucracy and a singular top–down approach to culture. However, as a way of redressing the balance we have closed with a case study to demonstrate how a well-considered top–down approach *can* work. By combining the two strategies of bottom–up and top–down, there is a much higher chance of success.

To close the chapter and this book we share a metaphor that compares culture change with lighting a bonfire. If the bonfire is lit only at the top, it will simply burn out. If the bonfire is lit at the top and *also* at various points at the base, we see the flames gradually engulfing each other and the fire will take off. Experimentation can become the catalyst... or the spark that ignites the fire.

Note

1 Hamel, G and Zanini, M (16 May 2017) Assessment: Do you know how bureaucratic your organization is?, *Harvard Business Review*, hbr.org/2017/05/assessment-do-you-know-how-bureaucratic-your-organization-is (archived at https://perma.cc/FP4Y-GY5G)

Afterword

Our aim, throughout this book, has been to provide insights into the philosophy of business experimentation as well as its methodology. Experience has taught us that, gaining the knowledge and learning the process is very often the easy part. The real difficulty is in adjusting the attitudes and mindsets that can play such an important role in shaping an 'experimental' culture. It is why we have taken a dual approach to the topic, providing both a practical guide and a conceptual proposition.

We have argued the case for business experimentation and its timeliness. We have described the process, prescribed tools and techniques, highlighted the pitfalls and explained ways to overcome them. We have viewed experimentation through the lenses of both the individual and the organization. Our intention has been to inform, inspire, provoke and challenge in equal measure. More than anything, we hope that it has provided you with the confidence and the tools to give experimentation a try.

In that sense, you might think of this book as a call to arms. There is an opportunity now that has rarely been there before, as businesses begin to recalibrate and re-examine their purpose in a post-pandemic world. But it is not just about reviewing strategies, product offerings or delivery channels. The way that people work together in the pursuit of a common cause needs rethinking. It is time to reinvent – and humanize – the workplace. How it will all be achieved remains uncertain, but experimentation can play an important part in helping with the answers.

We began the book with a quote from one of the greatest 20th-century scientists. We shall close with another of his astute observations:

The imagination of nature is far, far greater than the imagination of man.
Richard Feynman

If Feynman is correct, what might we learn from the 'imagination of nature'? The following parable provides us with an insight.

The parable of the bees

Karl von Frisch, a Nobel Prize-winning ethologist, studied bee cognition and how bees communicate with each other.[1] He discovered that when a bee comes across a rich source of nectar and pollen, it returns to the hive and performs a tell-tale dance for its fellow bees. The tale it tells conveys the coordinates of the precious food source by the waggle movements of its dance. But that is not all. A good proportion of the bees in a hive do not adhere to this waggle-dance routine by which familiar sources of food are fully exploited; instead, they act as explorers, randomly seeking out food sources beyond the familiar ones, albeit with little success most of the time.

So, we have two distinct forms of behaviour: there are the 'efficient' bees, staying loyal to a tried-and-tested habit, playing it safe, not straying too far from the hive, and securing reliable and beneficial outcomes; and there are the 'inefficient' bees, conducting trial-and-error reconnaissance sorties, venturing beyond the predictable, failing most of the time, but every now and then alighting, literally, on a major discovery. The health of the hive then depends upon this magical mix of exploitation and exploration, efficiency and waste, certainty and doubt, and order and anarchy. For bees, experimentation is not something that is switched on or off according to circumstances. It is a permanent feature of life in the hive.

But what relevance does this have for the organization? What lessons can be drawn?

Typically, it is only under perilous circumstances that companies invest in experimental solutions. The bureaucratic mind prefers to place its faith in planned and controlled responses to problems. This suggests that we've got the balance wrong. We need more exploration and less exploitation, not just in times of crisis but at all times. Sometimes we need to free ourselves from the illusion of certainty and our need for predictability so as to venture beyond the horizon of our familiar world. In other words, just like the bees, we may need to have more 'intrapreneurs' with an experimental mindset and fewer 'operators' with ready-made remedies.

The waggle-dance of managerialism, with its emphasis on the past and aspirations of control and certainty, can only take us so far; it needs to be supplemented by a strong commitment to experimentation, come rain or shine.

This is the message of this book.

Note

1 Von Frisch, K (1967) The Dance Language and Orientation of Bees, Belknap Press, Boston

APPENDIX A: THE SCIENCE OF BUSINESS EXPERIMENTATION

Throughout this book we have commented on a scientific approach to experimentation and described how the level of rigour increases in relation to the experiment's complexity. In a simple 'try it and see' experiment there is rarely a need to do more than observe the results and make decisions based on the observations. However, when experiments influence strategic or operational choices, decisions will demand greater confidence. It is here that a more robust, scientific approach to data collection is required.

A 'scientific' approach is not meant to suggest that business experiments are to be compared in the same light as clinical experiments. We use the term here to illustrate how, in more complex situations, greater attention needs to be paid to the experiment design and data collection. The level of rigour required is a regular challenge and will be different in every experiment. The best way to judge is to assess whether the results allow business decisions to be made with a 'reasonable degree of confidence'.

A good way of testing confidence is whether the same results and data would be reproduced if the experiment was repeated under the same conditions. In experiment terminology this is known as **reliability**. A second measure of confidence is how accurately the experiment has measured what it was meant to measure. In experiment terminology this is known as **validity**.

These are just two of the many terms that are used when we speak about a scientific approach to business experimentation. Here we aim to provide insights into that language by explaining different experiment design choices and by providing a 'glossary of terms'.

1. Experiment design choices

The early stages of the six-step process will influence the decision about the experiment design, but those choices can evolve even up to the hypothesis stage. It will be evident from the examples in the book that experiment design can take many forms. Yet we are often guilty of viewing them through a single lens. In this section we look at the variety of activities that can be captured under the umbrella of 'experimentation'.

a. Randomized control trials (RCT) (and A/B testing)

A/B testing is probably the most common form of experimentation in business and became popular with web designers and analysts at the turn of the millennium. Today it has reached new levels of sophistication as online businesses, like Amazon and Google, are constantly testing and measuring consumer data and preferences. This type of experiment design uses a control group and an experiment (or treatment) group, where the latter is subject to an intervention. The results are then compared after an agreed period. Because of the similarities, we often fall into the trap of using RCT and A/B testing interchangeably. It is, however, important to distinguish the difference. An RCT has a more formalized structure and design that relies upon a higher level of scientific rigour and provides a greater confidence in the results. It is this type of business experiment design that features in most of our examples.

b. Multivariate testing (MVT)

Multivariate testing has similar characteristics to A/B or RCT testing, but in this case there are multiple dependent variables. This may look like A/B1, B2, B3 where the experiment or treatment groups (B) are tested with three different versions of the intervention. They can be subtle variations on the same theme or very different options with the goal of determining which combination of variables performs the best. While this type of experiment is used a lot in web page design, it can also be a valuable tool in broader business experiments, as we illustrate below:

> The experiment team in an FMCG organization in France wanted to experiment with different ways of managing their supply chain of dairy products. In the DISCOVER and IDEATE stages they had produced three equally good improvement options they were keen to test. They had sufficient resources and capacity to set up a control group as well as three separate experiment groups. They were initially concerned about the additional rigour this required, particularly as each group had to be comparable, but went ahead and ran a closely monitored MVT as a first phase. The experiment results revealed that one option was not as good as originally thought, but separate parts of the other two options showed positive results. The team ran a second phase as an RCT with a hybrid option that combined the parts of the better two. The resulting data provided them with the confidence to implement the changes to the wider organization.

c. Proof of concept

Concept testing or 'proof of principle' can be a very simple experiment to measure initial customer reactions to a service or product without actually producing the product. It is widely used in marketing but can also be used in testing business models, pricing, promotions and customer experience. This type of experiment still demands a rigorous approach in the preparation stage to produce a realistic offering. A poorly researched concept is unlikely to get the desired response. That is why teams are encouraged to continue the discipline of developing a hypothesis. It not only helps with planning the experiment, but it can be critical in shaping the way in which the proposal or concept is framed.

> This was the case with a mid-sized IT support company in Germany. They had moved to a new centralized office and had an arrangement with a telecoms client to rent one of their previous offices. Not only

would they continue to provide IT support, but they also became a 'landlord', providing additional facilities management and concierge services. The arrangement was very profitable and led the IT company to explore whether this could be an additional line of service using other vacant offices. They had gained some idea that the concept could be profitable but that was with an existing client that met their specific needs at the time. They were not confident that it was sufficient proof to invest time and divert resources from their core business. They wanted to test the concept's attraction if it was packaged as a separate service offering to a wider population and they experimented in two phases. First, they built and refined an offering that was informed by discussions with one group of clients. Using that information, they developed a single concept with a detailed proposal and a tiered price structure that they used to test the concept with a second group of existing and potential clients. The results demonstrated that there *was* a market for the concept, but the level of desired profitability could only be achieved with a combined facilities management and IT support element. The proof of concept had not only saved a lot of money, but the information gained also allowed the IT company to add to the client service options among its support services.

d. Pilots, prototypes, MVPs and mock-ups

The proof of concept is aimed at testing an idea, whereas the four types of experiments we consider here are, in most cases, dealing with a *tangible* product or service. In each case the experiment aim is to present a 'taster' of the final version that can be developed using feedback loops from customers and end users.

PILOTS

Pilots are small-scale versions of a larger rollout. TV programmes are often produced as pilots to test audience reaction and make changes before investing in a longer series. As an effort to encourage the use of e-bikes, the UK government used a number of pilot schemes to build evidence to decide upon the most effective approaches before they allocated funds for a wider rollout in 2021.

PROTOTYPES AND MOCK-UPS

Prototypes and mock-ups are ways of testing a hypothesis by developing the product. In industries such as aerospace this can be a long-term and expensive process. In the automotive industry, 'concept cars' are examples of mock-ups and prototypes where ideas and drawings are physically transformed into a life-size object. The idea is that they can be gradually transformed into road cars. In a motor show the cars are likely to be *mock-ups* that are physically identical to the concept but may not be fully functional. Examples like the VW Golf was a road-ready *prototype* in 1969 and has seen an 'evolutionary' or 'incremental' process of product development ever since in its many guises. Prototypes do not need to be expensive, and manufacturers will often produce 'throwaway' versions in the early stages of design to test a product or a part simply to gain feedback.

MINIMUM VIABLE PRODUCTS

A minimum viable product (MVP) originates from lean startup methodology. The experiment's aim is to produce a product or service with the least effort that will still function sufficiently to gain maximum learning. It works on the premise that an actual product must be produced and offered to customers and their specific behaviour is observed. It means that the experiment can determine what they *really do* in using the product and becomes a more reliable way of soliciting feedback than asking what *they might do*.

POP-UPS

Pop-ups are similar to pilots in retail where a new service or product is launched and tested, typically in a shopping mall or short-term premises. The information gained can then be used to inform further investment.

2. The logic of an experiment

The seven choices described above are the most common examples of business experiments that we encounter. Most of the experiments in this book fit into the earlier categories of randomized control trials (RCT), multivariate trials (MVT) and concept testing. Here we use them to explain more about experiment terminology.

The skill of experimental design lies in the ability to systematically and precisely manipulate an independent variable(s) while accurately measuring the dependent variable(s):

The **independent variable** is the 'action' or 'intervention' that will be applied to cause an intended change.

The **dependent variable** is the desired outcome that needs to be measured before and after the experiment if it is to deliver a clear and unambiguous result.

A good experimental design is one in which the researcher is able to manage external influences to be confident that the changes in the dependent variable can only be due to the interventions. By examining the influence of one variable upon another, while excluding the influence of other variables, the managerial aim is to strengthen the rationality and evidence base. This means that key decisions made by the company are made through a greater understanding of cause–effect relationships.

In the ideal case, the truth of a hypothesis is discovered by comparing two groups:

- The experiment group is exposed to the intervention.
- The control group operates as normal.

For the experiment to be unbiased, it is crucial that the members of the experiment group and the control group are indistinguishable from each other. This means that, where possible, they must be randomly drawn from the same population and representative of a wider population if the experiment results are to be upscaled. Any differences between them must be due to chance.

3. Elements of experimental design

The process below explains the key stages of a randomized control experiment:

- A problem or opportunity is identified and researched to gain a better understanding of the issues.
- Using the early research, a hypothesis proposes a cause–effect relationship between two variables, the independent and dependent variables.
- The hypothesis takes the form, 'if action (X) is taken, then it will result in outcome (Y)'.
- X is the independent variable and Y is the dependent variable.
- Two groups (A/B) are formed, with the experiment group experiencing the intervention (X) and the control group operating as normal to provide the comparison.
- Baseline measures are taken with both groups at the start and again at the end of the experiment.
- The intervention is applied to the experiment group and not the control group.
- Both the control and experiment groups are protected from external influences.
- Any differences in the measures are assumed to result solely from the intervention (X) and will provide evidence to test whether the hypothesis is proven or disproven.
- Practical implications are drawn upon and business recommendations made.

FIGURE A.1 A process for experimentation

PROBLEM or OPPORTUNITY

INTERVENTION
Experiment group

Control group

EXPECTED OUTCOMES

MEASUREMENT POINTS

Researching the problem or opportunity and defining it clearly.

Validating the problem with clear data and evidence.

The intervention is experienced by the *experiment group*. It is the element being changed. It is an isolated activity known as the INDEPENDENT variable.

The control group is unchanged.

The intervention will impact the DEPENDENT variable(s).

Expected changes are stated in the hypothesis. The metrics and the criteria for success will determine a proven or unproven hypothesis.

HYPOTHESIS

4. Glossary of terms

There are a number of defining features and terms associated with business experimentation. We expand on them here to provide a point of reference:

Confidence: This is about the trust we should place in the findings of a particular experiment. It relates to the probability that the results of the experiment accord with the truth. A business experiment is usually a comparison between two states of affairs: the status quo and a new way of doing business.

Control: This stands for the concerted attempt by the researcher to eliminate any possible contamination of the relationship between the independent and dependent variables by external factors. There needs to be no doubt that the effect could not have been caused by any other variable than the independent variable of interest. This is achieved by the use of a control group.

Control group: A randomized group of people that are part of the experiment but not affected by the intervention. They operate as normal but also need to be protected from other 'external' influences that might impact upon the results.

Experiment group: This is the group that will experience the intervention (X) and their results will be compared directly with the control group to test the truth of the hypothesis.

External validity: This refers to the degree to which the results of an experiment can be upscaled or universalized. In other words, do the findings generalize to other people, other places and other times? Can the findings be inferred to the world beyond the experiment? An obvious way of boosting external validity is replication, conducting the same experiment but on different populations in different settings.

Hawthorne effect: This refers to the tendency of individuals to change their behaviour if they know that they are being observed and measured as participants in an experiment. For example, they may work harder or try to raise their game if they believe that they are being compared with others.

Internal validity: This refers to the degree to which an experiment demonstrates a trustworthy cause-and-effect relationship between a treatment and an outcome. Alternative explanations are rendered highly unlikely. Ways of strengthening internal validity include both randomization and 'blinding', that is, ensuring that the research subjects (and even the research team itself) do not know which subjects are in the experimental group and which are in the control group.

John Henry effect: This is when individuals who find themselves assigned to a control group perceive themselves to be at a 'competitive disadvantage' and treat this as a challenge to outperform the experimental group. This, of course, negates the experimental role that a control group is designed to play.

Manipulation: This refers to the purposeful and careful adjustment by the researcher of the independent variable with the aim of then observing the impact that this intervention has on the behaviour of the dependent variable of interest.

Randomization: This refers to the process whereby subjects are assigned either to the experimental group or to the control group. For the experiment to provide trustworthy findings, the subjects must be randomly assigned either to the experiment or to the control group.

Replication: This refers to the occasional need to repeat an experiment on a larger or more diverse group of subjects, particularly when only small samples have been used, so as to reduce the variability and increase the reliability of the test results. A single experiment may be insufficient to yield a robust finding.

Representative: A term linked with 'external validity'. The experiment and control groups must be representative of a wider population if there are plans to roll out the results to that population. This may impact particularly across different cultures and geographies.

Sample sizes: A term used to denote the number of people and/or locations involved. It links with statistical significance. The sample size needs to be large enough to produce sufficient and reliable data for decisions to be made with reasonable confidence.

Significance – practical: This relates to a *business* question: 'How strongly are we influenced by the result to make a business decision?' This is more about commercial judgement. Real-life business experiments are more likely to be the subject of error than lab-based experiments. Practical issues such as time constraints or external influences on the results can affect confidence in the outcomes.

Significance – statistical: This asks the question: 'How confident can we be that the result is not purely by chance?' It concerns precision and probability theory. Because an experiment, by definition, works with a small subset of the population, there will always be an issue of whether the behaviour of the sample can be safely extrapolated to the population from which it is drawn. This is a *scientific* question.

APPENDIX B: CASE STUDY:
LEARNING FROM OTHERS

Gerardo is a senior manager in financial services in Spain and wanted to change his client base from a reliance on high-volume, low-margin business to one of fewer clients but higher value and higher margins. The existing bonus reward system encouraged consultant behaviour that favoured the former and there was a strong loyalty to that well-established process. Previous attempts to change had ended in failure and Gerardo, new to the experimentation process, wanted to use it to try a different approach. Our work with other parts of the organization made us aware that managers in Germany had resolved a similar challenge. At the same time, different clients in an Indian HR consultancy were exploring new reward and performance systems for their teams and were already experimenting. Having exhausted other ideas and seeing a common thread, Gerardo was keen to speak with his colleague in Germany and we connected him with India. The result was that, even though the situations were not identical, Gerardo immediately had five new and different ways that the topic could be addressed, none of which had been considered by him and his team in the past.

In speaking with India, he realized that using an experimental approach could provide a different way of introducing the desired changes. Previously, he had tried to involve different levels of employees in the process. He encouraged 'change champions' and used a communication plan, but he realized that the previous solutions had always been generated by his own management team. Learning from India, he saw an experimental approach as a way of changing the process. Not only did he want the approach to involve several tiers of the organization, but he also saw it as an opportunity to generate even more ideas.

He decided to run a multivariate experiment in four carefully selected locations with comparable client profiles and revenues. He and his management team worked with an employee group to select two of the most favoured solutions for a new performance reward system from the ideas already generated from Germany, India and their own discussions. He had learned from India how they had used an employee group as part of their experiment that had been given the brief: 'Here's the issue… come up with *your* ideas and test one,' so that became an additional experiment group.

The teams ran their experiment over a four-month period with the four locations:

- Madrid – control group – current system but still encouraged to change;
- Barcelona – experiment with solution A;
- Valencia – experiment with solution B;
- Bilbao – experiment with solution from employee group.

The experiments ran independently to avoid cross-contamination, but Gerardo was keen that learning should be shared as the experiment progressed. The leaders in each location were the 'experiment team' and they met regularly to support and challenge each other about the process and the 'scientific rigour' required. After four months each team presented its findings to each other. It was agreed that a new process would be adopted, mainly as a result of the findings in Barcelona that also included proposals from those in Bilbao, which had started with a blank canvas.

As each of the major locations had been involved in the experiment process there was a greater sense of ownership by the consultants than in previous attempts to change the system. The agreed solution was implemented and has already been successful in creating a different balance in client profiles. Gerardo commented that among the successes there had also been some surprises in how an experimental approach can add value. When asked what tips he might pass on to others, he highlighted the following 'takeaways':

- how so many ideas from other sources were unexpectedly relevant to his own problem;
- how they also helped to reveal different perspectives and spark even more ideas;
- how an experimental approach was able to create ownership where 'normal' change techniques had failed in the past;
- how the answers to a problem can *also* be found within the organization – simply by engaging people in the process.

APPENDIX C: PEOPLE EXPERIMENTS

People experiments are a popular topic for a number of reasons. First, their internal focus means less risk is involved and they rarely demand the level of scientific rigour required in more complex experiments. Second, they can be more easily managed in a discrete business area. Finally, in addition to the business benefits, those involved usually have a personal stake in the outcome, resulting in higher engagement.

Here we categorize 'people' experiments under three general headings:

- *organizational culture;*
- *relationships and processes;*
- *talent management.*

The following list provides short descriptions of the initial questions that have inspired over 30 experiments in these categories.

1. Organizational culture

With its many dimensions, organizational culture is a rich source of experiment topics. Some of the most common themes are organizational attitudes to failure and risk and how a business can become more innovative. Perhaps encouraged by the discussions of an experimental mindset, the questions on Table C.1 are some that clients have formulated into hypotheses and then tested.

TABLE C.1   Organizational culture experiment questions

Organizational culture	Experiment questions
Dealing with failure and risk	• What would be the impact on organizational attitudes if we externalized our 'failures' (as in the airline industry)? • How can we institutionalize smart risk-taking when faced with regulatory constraints? • Can we use open discussion methodology to 'celebrate' mistakes and change attitudes to failure?
Encouraging innovation	• Can we improve product development by crowd-sourcing innovation through an app? • If we simplify our guidelines, can we increase the quality and quantity of our patent ideas? • Can we improve creativity by co-locating employees with other organizations? • Can we become more creative if we provide employees with time to use their 'slice of genius'?
Collaboration	• How can we mobilize cross-boundary teamworking to create a group value proposition? • What is the best technology to make us less federated and work together for client benefits? • Can we set up a knowledge exchange to share commercial information in emerging markets?

2. Relationships and processes

Exploring better ways of working and the challenges of leadership and team effectiveness are regular features in 'people' experiments. They are popular because they are usually relevant to the 'day job' and have outcomes that have a personal impact. While some examples in Table C.2 can be complex, others, such as stand-up meetings, are easily set up and managed. Many of the experiments in the table have been a good way for experimentalists to start using the six-step process.

TABLE C.2   Relationships and processes experiment questions

Relationships and processes	Experiment questions
Leadership behaviours	• How will strategic thinking be improved if we used a behavioural cognitive tool as a prompt? • Will transparency of 360 feedback have an impact on leadership behaviours? • What would be the effect on leadership behaviours if we 'reverse-mentored'?
Team effectiveness	• Do peer-managed teams perform better than hierarchical ones? • Can 'youth' contributions add diversity and influence management team decisions?
Flexible working and lifestyle	• What type of flexible working will most improve our performance and productivity? • Could we provide optional accommodation to avoid long commutes (China and USA)? • Will implementing a 'life navigation' programme increase engagement and motivation?
Process and efficiency	• What would be the benefits if we have an email-free day once a week? • Will a 'concierge' system work to manage the volume and priorities of email? • What might be the advantages if we had all our meetings standing up? • Do virtual meetings really provide benefits over face-to-face/other options? (pre-2020)

3. Talent management

This section of 'people' experiments includes every part of the career journey, from recruitment, through career planning and on to retention and engagement. Once again, these are topics in which those experimenting have a personal interest. Their frequency among clients provides an interesting insight into the common organizational challenges that are found across a variety of industries.

TABLE C.3   Talent management experiment questions

Talent management	Experiment questions
Ratings and feedback	• What would be the impact if annual performance ratings were replaced by more regular performance discussions? • Can we use a mobile feedback app to improve the quality of performance feedback? • How can we use technology to make providing and seeking feedback an easy part of our daily work life?
Career management	• How can we make international assignments even more valuable to the individual and the organization? • Will changing the style and focus of job advertisements increase the quantity and quality of applicants? • What can we do to produce an optimal resourcing model that supports career development?
Engagement and motivation	• Will engagement improve if customer site visits are arranged for production teams to view user benefits? • What interventions will be most successful in retaining key staff members? • How can we motivate our middle managers in the same way as senior managers? • How can we increase our employee buy-in to the group strategy?

APPENDIX D: WHERE DO GAME-CHANGING IDEAS COME FROM?

It is a well-known truth that the more successful a firm is, the more blinkered its employees tend to be. Existing activities, capabilities and customer relationships drive behaviour, and things that are peripheral to its existing trajectory get filtered out.

So if you work in an established, successful firm, how do you expand your horizons? Where do you look and who do you talk to, if you want to access ideas that lie outside your existing areas of strength? If you ask anyone already linked to your firm, they may be as tainted and blinkered as you are. And there is always a risk they just tell you what they think you want to hear – or that you only hear the parts of the story that affirm your prior beliefs.

This was the puzzle that a team of Roche executives (Sven Ebert, Chad Brown, Tracy Bush, Greg Essert, Oliver Froescheis and Feng Wang) confronted in May 2014. 'We wanted to help Roche avoid the failure of success syndrome; we wanted to gain access to the *next* big ideas, not the ones we are currently working on,' observed Sven Ebert.

They formulated their question as follows: *Are we missing out on the disruptive or unconventional ideas – the true game-changers – that will let us reach our purpose?* And they hit upon a novel way of answering it: 'We had the bright idea to ask the next generation – the current graduate students, people untainted by our company and its biases, with (hopefully) a fresh point of view.'

Their initial thinking was to conduct some sort of student survey. 'We wanted to find really young scientists who are not influenced by a corporate mindset yet, who have got a really open mind regarding any game-changer which can occur in a 10–20-year timeframe.' The hypothesis was that by sourcing ideas from these emerging scientists, they would identify promising opportunities for Roche that were incremental to those identified using the established scouting process.

Finding the right people to ask

So far so good. But the team realized it wouldn't be easy to find these students – it would take too long to go through their own networks, and indeed there was a risk that everyone in their networks was drinking from the same 'Kool Aid' fountain.

The first solution was to send a survey to a group of MBA students from London Business School. But it flopped. 'We got so few responses, just two or three answers, it was nothing. It was an important learning point actually, because then we knew we had to do something different in order to really have a broad global reach.'

One of the team suggested using a third party, Oxbridge Biotech Roundtable (OBR), a company Roche had worked with before. OBR was a corporate-university networking organization, and it turned out to be the perfect partner. 'We already had some projects going on with OBR. One colleague said, hey, they have some experience with students and they bring industry and students together and they might be able to help you.'

A challenge was issued to OBR's network of thousands of students around the world: 'Do you have an idea for a groundbreaking innovation? Submit your idea by 12th September, fly to Basel and present to Roche, and win the prestigious £5,000 Game Changing Innovation prize.' OBR promised good visibility; for example, it found its way onto the homepage of MIT's pharmacy department, where the graduate students couldn't miss it.

Once the students clicked through, they were asked a set of specific questions: *What do you imagine will be the biggest healthcare need in 10 to 20 years? Please describe the background to the problem or opportunities you are seeking to address. Please describe your proposed innovation and specifically describe how this innovation would improve human health. If your innovation pertains to a product or service, describe how the final product or service would look.* 'We devised these questions to help the thinking process,' explained Sven Ebert. 'We set the ground first and then got to a specific innovation and then how it might be realized.'

After the failure of their first attempt, it was nerve-wracking waiting to see if there were any worthwhile responses, compounded by the fact that they launched it during the summer period. 'After four weeks we only had about 15 replies, but then as the deadline loomed the answers came rolling in. By 12th September we had 138 responses.' In total, OBR had sent out 7,856 emails and contacted 93 universities in 28 countries. The majority of the replies were from Europe, with some from North America and then a few from other parts of the world.

So the first goal – tapping into a body of students who didn't know Roche – had been achieved. And the team were pleasantly surprised at the feedback they got from the universities that participated. 'I think Roche deserves credit for a fresh perspective, and for giving young people an opportunity to throw in some creative and daring ideas,' said one.

The team conducted some initial analysis on the responses just by reading them through. By their reckoning, 48 per cent of the submissions were outside Roche's existing areas of focus. Major categories of submissions included continuous monitoring, big data, drug delivery and health apps.

Evaluating the submissions

The Roche team members each evaluated all 138 submissions using 5 criteria developed in consultation with internal technology assessment experts (how novel, how useful, etc), then they met up for a day to discuss the top 18, eventually coming up with 3 finalists. One key criterion was that the idea was genuinely new. 'One submission from an MIT student turned out to be him working as part-time marketing director for a startup. It was a great idea, but he was already commercializing it.'

The three finalists – one each from the UK, Slovenia and California – were invited to Basel to present to an internal panel of Roche experts. 'To be honest we were unsure if they would give good presentations or not. Our concerns were unwarranted – all three presenters performed very well,' recalls Sven Ebert. The winner was Jahir Gutyierrez from California, for 3D bioprinted smart red blood cells. 'It was a pretty unusual idea, that's basically why it won.' The UK finalist was working on detecting Alzheimer's at an early stage, using classic mobile phone games to see how reaction time and certain brain parameters change over time. The Slovenian finalist was proposing a new way to give medicine to the body via a skin patch. The team were clear throughout the process that only non-confidential information should be presented, to avoid any IP problems.

Learning and follow-up

So what was the outcome from this experiment? The internal Roche panel were extremely positive: 'I am convinced we need to get outside in order to overcome our focus on doing what we need today. We need more engagement. We must operationalize this,' said one.

From the team's point of view there were several linked findings. First, the study opened people's eyes to ideas – some very specific ones, but more importantly to entire categories of things that are growing. As Sven Ebert explained, 'Health apps or websites are one of the major drivers for our young people in the future, and not really rated at the right priority. And 3D printing is more important than we probably think at the moment. These emerging categories are really important.'

There were other benefits as well – one was good PR with universities, who liked the initiative. It was also a massive talent scouting opportunity. All the top 18 participants were approached by Roche HR people in their respective countries, and several job offers ensued.

There are plans to repeat the experiment in coming years, to keep the fresh ideas rolling in, and to avoid Roche scientists from becoming too inwardly focused. 'In the end, who knows how Roche's business model will look 20 years from now? At the moment, we think personalized medicine is going to be huge, but what happens if the rules really change fundamentally somehow? We need to make sure our early-warning system is working well, to make sure we stay relevant.'

With thanks to Professor Julian Birkinshaw,
London Business School

APPENDIX E: CASE STUDY: PAY WHAT YOU WANT

One of the most profound changes brought about by the Internet revolution is product pricing. For example, Priceline.com pioneered the idea that prices might be set by buyers rather than sellers, eBay brought auction-based pricing into the mainstream, Spotify charges for access, not ownership, and many online providers from LinkedIn to the *New York Times* use a 'freemium' model, where the basic service is free but you pay for premium content.

How about a pay-what-you-want pricing model? It sounds pretty risky to rely on the goodwill of customers to pay more than they have to, ie nothing, but it seems to work in some settings. One early pioneer was the band Radiohead, which reportedly made $3 million in a year from asking customers to pay what they wanted for a download of their album *In Rainbows*. Various restaurants, musicians and charities have experimented with their own versions of this model.

But how far can the pay-what-you-want model be stretched? Does it only work for digital products, where the marginal cost of production is zero? Or is there room to try it out in a more traditional industry setting?

That was the question a group of executives from Swiss healthcare company, Roche, asked themselves (team members were Jan Schreiber, Katarzyna Stadnicka, Maik Roeck, Rae Ann Farrow, Raj Harapanahalli and Jean Eric Charoin). Last year, they designed and ran a simple experiment where they piloted a pay-what-you-want approach for a diagnostic test, in some German pharmacies and Italian GP surgeries. Their experiment had some fascinating and surprising results that open up important questions about how certain types of healthcare services are provided.

The experiment had its origins in an executive development programme in 2015. Jan Schreiber explained:

> The idea came from two things coming together. I had read an article about new types of pricing models and how they might influence companies, especially in the digital world. And around the same time, I had a discussion with a colleague about a diagnostic product they wanted to launch here in Germany, where they were worried about how to price it. So when I talked to my team members, out came the crazy idea: why not test a pay-what-you-want model in a diagnostic setting?

The device in question was a point-of-care blood test for two cardio-vascular risk factors, lipid levels and three months' average glucose levels (HbA1c). In Germany, these tests were traditionally done by the GP taking blood from a vein and sending it off to a lab to be checked. Now, using this new device, the patient could get a quick finger prick, put some drops of blood on a test disc, and be presented with the results 15 minutes later.

While it was a neat innovation, getting doctors to change the habits of a lifetime was proving difficult, not least because the financial incentives worked in the opposite direction: health insurance covered the costs of lab tests, but small devices like these were reimbursed at a very low level. 'As the GP market in Germany was not attractive, we planned to address the pharmacies and the growing market of people taking care for their own health with an innovative pricing concept,' explained Schreiber.

The team identified 10 suitable pharmacies in Germany, and they convinced Roche's sales head in that region to support the experiment with two sales reps. Two sales reps were then trained to give the pharmacists detailed instructions. A key point was that the pharmacists should not say the service was free; instead, they were instructed to say, 'We will do this service, and at the end you can decide what you want to pay.' They also decided to loan the instrument to the pharmacies at no cost, all in the interests of getting quickly to the nub of the experiment, which was to understand patient behaviour in the pay-what-you-want condition. The hypothesis, of course, was that the pay-what-you-want model might bring in less revenue per test but with higher overall usage – which, for a product designed to fore-warn people about risk conditions, could only be a good thing.

As people in Germany are not used to paying for diagnostic tests, the team offered two different anchor prices (€15/€25) to five pharmacies each, so that if a customer asked how much the price would usually be, the pharmacist could reveal this piece of information.

How did the experiment work out? Over the three-month test period, 235 people used the service in the pay-what-you-want condition. Fifteen per cent paid nothing, the other 85 per cent paid anything from €1 to €25, with an average of €6.65. 'For us it was very interesting that people paid almost as much for one test – either lipids (€6.47) or HbA1c (€5.01) – as for both tests together,' explained Schreiber. 'So doing only one test each time has the potential to increase sales significantly, plus it reduces time to result by about 50 per cent.' The anchor prices also played a part, with a third of people paying €15 and one in four paying €25.

The team also tried a version of the experiment in Italy, and because of the different reimbursement rules there it made sense to do it with GP surgeries. They ended up with 86 people using the service across 8 GP surgeries. The anchor price here was €35, 'because Italians are used to paying €60 or more for these types of services as part of an annual check-up'. Of this sample, 23 per cent paid nothing, but the average price paid was €19.25, with people paying anything from €5 to €35. The equivalent figure in the Italian control sample was €23.

So what did the team learn? Perhaps not surprisingly, the pay-what-you-want model resulted in a slightly lower price being paid, because some people chose to pay nothing. The team also learned a lot about framing the pricing decision. 'We sought feedback from the pharmacists and GPs in terms of the right words to use. Some people were a bit too shy to sell the extra service, so our salespeople were very useful here, providing them guidance, showing them how to do it.'

But the whole point of the experiment was about increasing the accessible market. Schreiber noted that 'this was a pricing model no one had used before, so we were very excited about the good results'. While a pay-what-you-want model isn't likely to work in the long term here, a freemium model might have legs, with a basic test for free and then a higher price for the more complete service.

And of course there is a bigger picture story here, with Roche, like many other healthcare companies, seeking to help people take responsibility, understand their risk conditions, and adapt their lifestyle accordingly. As Schreiber observed:

> We had 24 people (8 per cent) in our study for whom we detected high levels of lipids or glucose levels, but they hadn't known about it. They wouldn't have taken the test with standard pricing, but now they are empowered to take the next steps to reduce their cardiovascular risk. Imagine rolling this out, and testing not 300 people but 30,000 people. The benefits to society are potentially huge.

So how is Roche using the results of this experiment? The team is working with executives in the diagnostics business unit to see if a version of this experiment can be trialled more widely. Clearly, this pricing model only works in certain parts of the medical system, but the core idea – that novel approaches to pricing can have a significant effect on customer behaviour – is one with enormous applicability across a range of settings. As Jan Schreiber says, 'Don't try to figure out at your office desk what a good price is. Go to the market, experiment and get a result. You might be surprised by what you learn. Then adapt your price accordingly.'

With thanks to Professor Julian Birkinshaw,
London Business School

APPENDIX F: THE INTERNAL MARKET AS A CHOICE ARCHITECTURE

The shadow organization

This is the design document that we drew up to present the experiment to the senior management, written in a purposefully polemical manner:

Diagnosis

The problem is not VUCA (an environment that is volatile, uncertain, complex, ambiguous), but FIFA, an organizational culture that is:

- Frenetic – we are busy fools… we are chasing short-term goals.
- Indecisive – we procrastinate… we kick the can down the road.
- Fearful – we dream vaguely, but dread precisely.
- Alienated – we are dispirited… we are not being true to ourselves.

Remedy

The emphasis needs to be placed differently:

- on business, not just busyness;
- on outcomes, not just intentions;
- on deeds, not just words;
- on reality, not just rhetoric;
- on authenticity, not 'bad faith' (Sartre's phrase for when we disown our innate freedom).

Inputs

- **Not:** just another set of academic lectures or expert opinions or noble intentions or corporate credos.

But:

- a down-to-earth action programme;
- a single, big, newsworthy idea;
- contagious and addictive; and
- unique to the company.

The design principles

- A **shadow organization** is created in which the future is invented.
- This is an organization dedicated to designing and conducting experiments as the foundation of its future success.
- It consists of small, self-selecting, self-organizing teams coming together to transform the company through continuous experimentation.
- The volunteer members of this organization have 'skin in the game'.
- This is not time taken away from the business; it is time invested more creatively and conscientiously in the business.
- No one has been 'sent' on the programme; everyone has elected to join it.
- The motto is: 'Whoever tries the most stuff wins.'

The nature of the shadow organization

- It operates more like a marketplace than a hierarchy.
- It feels more like a startup than a bureaucracy.
- It scorns standard processes and discourages compliant behaviour.
- It models a learning organization.
- Motto: 'Think big, start small, learn fast.'

The core idea

- A random sample of 150 employees are invited to respond to a challenge set by the chief executive.
- The challenge takes the form of a question: 'What is the problem to which we need brilliant solutions if we are to accelerate our transformational process?'
- The answers to this question, as given by each of the 150 participants, are shared, and they all then vote on which problems(s) they would most like to work on.
- Through negotiation, those who want to become active members of this shadow organization form into teams of five members, with each team selecting the problem that most attracts them.
- Everyone now has skin in the game working on self-chosen issues that they find important and interesting.
- From the population of 150, one might expect to have, say, 20 teams of 5 signing up to 20 key issues.
- The teams use experimentation to answer their chosen problem.

The sequence of activities

- The letter of invitation, setting out the challenge, is sent to the target population.
- The answers to the question are gathered.
- By a voting process, the participants form into teams, each with their own issue.
- A webinar is designed to explain the aims, structure and style of the ensuing programme of activity.
- Teams go to work on their experiments, refining the question, formulating hypothetical solutions, designing and conducting the experiments.
- As the teams go to work, so the network of cooperation expands, so the circle of trust develops, so the contagion strengthens, so the

confidence grows, and so the new behaviours become natural and embedded within this newly emerging organization.

- Gradually the old organization morphs into the new; the shadow organization serves to exemplify new, more experimental ways of working; and a 'post-bureaucratic' organization comes into being.

Summary

- Nothing is taught, apart from the principles of experimentation.
- A setting is created in which different behaviours and a new culture emerge naturally.

The OpenMarket

This is the design document that was the basis of our proposal.

Basic precepts

- Managers learn more by doing than deliberating, particularly those with the greatest potential.
- Markets outperform hierarchies, particularly in turbulent times that call for entrepreneurship.
- Teams can be wiser than individuals, particularly if they are cross-disciplinary groups of diverse talents.
- Crowds can be cleverer than experts, particularly when it comes to predicting the future.

Choice architecture

- The 'rules of the game' – how the OpenMarket operates – are published.
- Five internal venture capital banks are formed, each staffed by five managers drawn from different functions, levels and businesses

within the company, and possibly including one 'outsider' (such as a key customer).

- Each bank is allocated an initial capital fund of £500,000.
- All managers not on the executive board are invited to participate as 'players' in the OpenMarket.
- Participation is entirely voluntary.
- The role of the business school is to facilitate and enrich the process – through the occasional workshop, a permanent but light element of team coaching, and helpful suggestions of contacts, readings and benchmarks.

Business purpose

- to strengthen and accelerate the process of innovation within the company;
- to test the idea that an internal market in ideas, talent and funding outperforms a traditional hierarchy when it comes to the pace of successful innovation, whether in relation to the company's business model or organization model;
- in so doing, to develop an appetite and aptitude for large-scale organizational experimentation.

Experimental design

- Participants who want to 'play' organize themselves into diverse teams of five members.
- Over a period of no more than four weeks, each team formulates a radical idea for improving the performance of the company.
- When they have an idea worth sharing and testing, they sign up for a two-day workshop.
- Each workshop brings four or five teams together for two days to bring the ideas to a level of quality and originality that earns each team the right to pitch their idea to the internal venture capital banks.

- These workshops use the presentational technique of Pecha Kucha, a storytelling technique,[1] to turn the ideas into powerful investment proposals.

- Teams pitch their ideas and their request for capital to the internal banks of their choice.

- Each bank decides whether or not to invest in the ideas brought to them for consideration – and on what terms.

- The banks themselves are in competition with each other. Each bank knows that their funds are finite – and that therefore they have to choose carefully between the ideas submitted to them.

- Prior to this, the banks themselves will have attended workshops to help them develop their lending skills, apply investment criteria and formulate their own strategy for competing with each other.

- The bankers are rewarded in proportion to the performance of their loan portfolios.

- Teams whose ideas get funding can sign up for a second two-day workshop.

- These workshops bring together four or five 'winning teams' to work on the practical issues of bringing their idea to market efficiently and effectively.

- Teams take responsibility for helping each other to succeed by asking questions and listening to advice.

- The expectation is that the OpenMarket will financially outperform the 'official' or 'normal' method of innovation within the company, as well as preparing managers for senior executive roles more effectively than the standard business school programme.

Note

1 www.pechakucha.com (archived at https://perma.cc/9JWJ-DZ7N)

How do you embrace the full benefits of new technology without eroding a business model that depends so much on relationships and personal contact? It is a question faced by many 'people' businesses and, in early 2017, Randstad, the global recruitment company, was no different. In the 57 years since its foundation, Randstad had built its reputation on values that promoted trust and customer intimacy. From a small office in Amsterdam, those principles had seen it grow to become the global No. 2 in the staffing industry, operating in 39 countries with 38,000 employees. This case study explains how an engaged leadership driving a transformational initiative helped them towards the global No. 1 spot.

With improved data science, artificial intelligence and increasingly automated hiring systems, the adoption of new technology in the staffing business was accelerating faster than most other industries. Jacques van den Broek, the CEO, and his executive board knew that they had to keep pace and to get ahead where possible. They recognized they had a choice. Randstad could either be disrupted by technology and competition, or they could help Randstad disrupt itself by creating a transformational journey of their own making. At the same time, they knew that the Randstad DNA, with its emphasis on humanist values and a strong focus on execution and high performance, had to be preserved. Their answer was an initiative designed to accelerate success in the new digital reality.

As the 'Tech and Touch' strategy was introduced, it was clear to Jos Schut, Randstad's Global Chief Human Resources Officer (CHRO), and Michelle Prince, SVP Global Head of Learning and Development (SVP L&D), that for the initiative to fulfil its potential, it would mean changing established leadership behaviours and long-held managerial practices. It would mean cultivating a more innovative and collaborative culture to embrace new ways of working. Led from the top, Randstad partnered with London Business School (LBS) to design and deliver a 9-month programme for over 120 senior managers in 7 cohorts – the Transformational Leadership Programme (TLP).

Randstad wanted to place business experimentation at the heart of the programme and use it as a catalyst for change. They wanted participants to examine their own leadership behaviours and address their day-to-day challenges through an experimental approach. The aim was for Randstad leaders to share their learning with others as part of the experiment experience and for that learning to be diffused across the organization. As the programme sponsors, the CHRO and SVP L&D were aware of the limitations of a top–down approach by itself. They knew that, for it to succeed and to create sustainable change, it needed more than distant exhortations from above. It was clear, though, that the CEO and executive board were not simply supportive, but fully committed to drive both the initiative and the TLP forward through engaged and motivated leadership. This case study provides an illustration of how cultural change using experimentation as a catalyst can be led from above.

Engaged leadership

- **Launch webinars.** The CHRO and SVP L&D were part of 1.5-hour launch webinars with LBS on each programme to explain the *why*. This included the business rationale for the initiative but, from an experiment perspective, it also introduced senior managers to the desired behaviours. The senior managers attending were also asked to begin to consider opportunities or problems for experiment topics.

- **CEO and executive board involvement.** It had long been a tradition in Randstad for the CEO and executive board (EB) members to take an active role in leadership development programmes, and the

TLP was no exception. At least one EB member attended each in-person module at LBS and were further involved in leading two inter-modular webinars as part of the programme. This meant they were able to gain insights into experiment topics and provide feedback to participants at an early stage. With the involvement of EB members and with the CEO joining every group, it created frequent opportunities to discuss business performance and cultural change in an informal setting.

- **Senior-level sponsors.** Every experiment topic was supported by an EB member or senior executive as its sponsor. This meant that they would act as both a coach and a 'client' to ensure that the experiment had the potential to add measurable value throughout the nine months.

- **Experiment value and learning.** Approximately four months after each programme, every experiment group presented their findings to the CEO and EB. In addition to the outcomes and proposed next steps, the experiment teams shared their learning. These sessions became important for the experiment teams to hear the experiences of others; to discover the common challenges and successes of an experimental approach to business decision-making beyond their experiences.

- **Continuity.** The TLP was just part of a wider organizational initiative, but momentum was maintained around the experiment experiences by scheduled conversations with the CEO and EB long after programme completion. The meetings were not only an opportunity to update progress on the experiment outcomes, but also for a conversation about the behavioural and leadership aspects of culture change.

The experiment experience

The CHRO and SVP L&D were aware at the start that simply 'training' a tier of 120 senior managers would never be enough to create the changes they desired, but it was a starting point. They saw experimentation, with all its ambiguities and uncertainties, as a way of preparing participants for the future. It would provide a 'safe' environment for them to take risks, try out different behaviours and ways of working with colleagues. The overall aim was to help them to become more comfortable with being uncomfortable. They also saw the TLP experience as a way of creating connections and building networks to encourage greater collaboration among the global leadership population. Thus, the programme combined a number of elements to create a catalyst for change. Using experimentation as its central theme, it provided a vehicle to diffuse the knowledge and mindsets in the wider organization in the following way:

- The experiment process required participants to try out new behaviours and different ways of working. It required them to question and discuss their attitudes to topics like 'failure' and risk. The disruptive nature of each business experiment created an unsettled environment that emulated real life but where risks could be managed.

- Each country or area representation had its managing director and between two and four colleagues from their senior team (OpCo) participate in the TLP. Their first responsibility on returning was to share the experience and what they learned with others in the OpCo that did not attend.

- In this way, the experiment became the responsibility of the wider OpCo. In almost all cases, it also involved other organizational specialists, such as marketing or finance. In this way the core 'experiment group' that would conduct the experiment was widened.

- Others in the country or business unit were then involved as part of the experiment itself. In some cases, this was as part of an experiment or control group. In other cases, those conducting the experiment involved colleagues in surveys, workshops and ideation sessions. In this way the experiment experience was being spread within the wider organization.

The leader as a teacher

In addition to the TLP, Randstad also launched a broader learning initiative: Leading Transformation in the Digital Age (LTDA). This was a digital version of the LBS experience, to local leaders and managers to spread the messages of innovation and experimentation across a wider population of managers and employees. Supported by LBS, its aim was to cascade the content from the 'senior' programme and reinforce the behaviours associated with this new culture of agility, innovation and collaboration. The objective was that those involved in the Transformational Leadership Programme became mentors and guides on the digital programme. Thus, leaders became 'teachers' by sharing their experiences of experimentation and how it could be used to enhance performance. With leaders operating as coaches and mentors, it also meant that they were role-modelling the desired behaviours among their own teams. This resulted in an experimentation and transformational mindset being instilled across the entire company. As new technology, tools and processes aligned with the Tech and Touch business strategy were rolled out, this became an important enabler.

Between 2019 and 2020 the LTDA involved over 1,200 managers who were supported globally by over 130 OpCo senior managers as mentors. The programme continues with the senior leadership continuing to provide momentum.

In 2019, Randstad was ranked No. 1 in the Staffing Industry Analysts' Largest Global Staffing Firms list.

INDEX

Printed in Great Britain
by Amazon

37320195R00152